OSPREY COMBAT AIRCRAFT · 66

C-47/R4D SKYTRAIN UNITS OF THE PACIFIC AND CBI

SERIES EDITOR: TONY HOLMES

OSPREY COMBAT AIRCRAFT · 66

C-47/R4D SKYTRAIN UNITS OF THE PACIFIC AND CBI

DAVID ISBY

OSPREY
PUBLISHING

Front cover

On 10 December 1943, C-47-DL 41-38721 *Lawton Limited/PAT* of the 2nd Troop Carrier Squadron (TCS) departed its base at Dinjan, in India, as part of a six-aircraft formation tasked with dropping supplies to Allied troops at Kajitu, near Fort Hertz, in Burma. The aircraft was crewed by 1Lt Charles B Lawton (pilot), 2Lt George J Laben (co-pilot), 1Lt Leo DeRuntz (navigator), 1Lt Joseph Feldman (radio), Sgt Louis Liotino (crew chief) and two unidentified 'pushers and kickers'.

As the aircraft approached the drop zone, with 41-38721 third in a line-astern formation, they were intercepted by a number of Japanese Army Air Force Ki-43 'Oscars' (misidentified as Zeros) from the 1st Chutai's 50th Sentai, based at nearby Myitkyina. Co-pilot 2Lt Laben recalled what happened next;

'There were 12 of them. They hit us as we were getting ready to drop on Kajitu, and one C-47 was quickly knocked down. I looked out the side window and saw what I thought was an AT-6 Texan with fire coming out the front of it. I said to Chuck Lawton, "What's an AT-6 doing out here shooting at us?" He was lined up on the C-47 in front of us, which was the aircraft shot down. Chuck yelled, "That's no AT-6, that's a Zero", and we peeled off. He said, "I'll work the controls, you keep the throttle prop pitch full forward and keep me posted on the instrument readings". We instructed the food droppers to dump the load, which they did in record time.

'Leo DeRuntz kept us posted on where the Zeros were by going from rear side windows to the navigator's dome. I think we had a Zero after us at least three different times. On the last one, he had us lined up pretty good. Chuck dived down sharply and we were well over the airspeed instrument red lines. Then, at the last second, he pulled up sharply over a small mountain ridge. The Zero apparently didn't see the ridge and hit the top of it. The food droppers in the back said they saw it explode. We didn't go back to find out. We continued hedge-hopping through the mountains to the Hukwang valley and then through the mountains north of Shingbwiyan onto Ledo, before finally making it back to Dinjan.'

First published in Great Britain in 2007 by Osprey Publishing
Midland House, West Way, Botley, Oxford, OX2 0PH
443 Park Avenue South, New York, NY, 10016, USA
E-mail; info@ospreypublishing.com

ISBN 978 1 84603 046 8

Edited by Tony Holmes
Page design by Tony Truscott
Cover Artwork by Mark Postlethwaite
Aircraft Profiles by Chris Davey and Scale Drawings by Mark Styling
Index by Alan Thatcher
Originated by PDQ Digital Media Solutions
Printed and bound in China through Bookbuilders

07 08 09 10 11   10 9 8 7 6 5 4 3 2 1

For a catalogue of all books published by Osprey please contact:
NORTH AMERICA
Osprey Direct, C/o Random House Distribution Center,
400 Hahn Road, Westminster, MD 21157
E-mail:info@ospreydirect.com

ALL OTHER REGIONS
Osprey Direct UK, P.O. Box 140 Wellingborough, Northants, NN8 2FA, UK
E-mail: info@ospreydirect.co.uk
www.ospreypublishing.com

Dedication
For Dr Fredrick Raucher ('Uncle Fred'), a veteran of both sides of the 'Hump', who made every flight an adventure and enjoyed every meal

Both Lawton and Laben (with 235 combat missions and more than 1000 combat hours to his credit) survived their time in the CBI, while 41-38721 duly acquired a kill marking which made it one of the most famous C-47s in the CBI. The Ki-43 that had crashed whilst attacking the transport had been flown by Warrant Officer Oshima, who failed to return to base. Part of the original equipment of the 2nd TCS, the C-47 was written off on 28 July 1944 at Dinjan when an attached pilot retracted the landing gear by mistake when taxiing on the runway. 41-38721 had logged some 2400 flying hours by the time of its demise (*Cover artwork by Mark Postlethwaite*)

CONTENTS

DEVELOPMENT AND EARLY WAR SERVICE

In the Pacific and China-Burma-India (CBI) theatres of World War 2, military versions of the Douglas DC-3 airliner – most notably Army Air Force C-47/53s and Navy/Marine Corps R4Ds – enabled the advance of Allied ground and air forces in New Guinea and Burma, resupplied China from India and dropped paratroops in New Guinea, the Philippines and Burma. These aircraft delivered supplies, flew cargo to forward bases to maintain bombers and repair warships, evacuated wounded and made a powerful contribution in achieving victory.

The first truly modern airliners, introduced during the 1930s, embodied technological innovations that would subsequently shape combat aircraft in World War 2. They were multi-engined land-based aeroplanes of all metal construction, with constant-speed propellers, deicers and radio navigation aids. In worldwide service with airlines (while air arms across the globe still operated fabric-covered biplanes) were the Douglas DC-2, as well as the improved Douglas Sleeper Transport (DST) and DC-3.

The DC-3 first flew in 1935, this aircraft being an enlarged and up-engined version of the DC-2. In just a few short years, DC-3s brought about great improvements in airline services worldwide by being able to carry 21 passengers at some 200 mph.

The underfunded US military of the 1930s recognised the innovative technology embodied in these airliners but could only afford to procure them in small numbers. The US Army Air Corps (USAAC) used a few military transport versions of the DC-2 and DST (some with bigger fuselage cargo doors and reinforced flooring) as C-32/33/34s and C-39s, respectively. And although USAAC doctrine stressed the importance of

The C-39 was the military transport version of the Douglas Sleeper Transport (DST), which was also unofficially known as the 'DC-2^1/$_2$'. It was instrumental in building up the USAAC's pre-war transport operations capabilities. The two C-39s in the Philippines on 7 December 1941 escaped to Australia, where they were reinforced by other C-39s shipped in from the USA. These aircraft provided critical support to Allied operations in the region in the dark days of 1942 (*Author's Collection*)

air power's theatre-wide mobility, this led to little investment in transport aircraft. Senior officers believed that bombers could function as transports if required, while shorter range fighters would have to travel disassembled aboard ships to overseas destinations.

The Navy and Marine Corps also bought just a handful of off-the-shelf airliners, despite the former stressing forward sea and air bases but not investing in transport aircraft to make them operationally sustainable. The Marine Corps, however, had small-war experience with transports in Latin America, where one aircraft could replace a long and vulnerable column of pack animals or save wounded troops by air evacuation from forward airstrips.

US Army troops load a 37 mm anti-tank gun aboard a C-33 transport during large-scale manoeuvres held in the summer of 1941. Although these particular airlifts did not generate specific doctrine or the tactics, techniques and procedures that were needed to guide the airlift of Australian and US ground forces to New Guinea in 1942, they did provide inspiration. The C-33 was a modified DC-2 airliner with a large cargo door and reinforced floor. The transformation of the DC-2 into the C-33 gave Douglas the confidence to convert the DC-3 into the C-47 (*National Archives*)

The first USAAC DC-3 versions were the 'one-off' VIP-configured C-41 and C-41A. And although the USAAC had limited DC-3 experience pre-war, US-based airlines were using them effectively in all weathers literally across the country (*National Archives*)

The importance of transport aircraft, and the airborne assaults by parachute and glider they enabled, during the German offensives in Europe in 1940 changed US military policies, however. The US Army and Marine Corps hastily formed their own paratroop units that same year, following German and British examples.

Although gliders were initially seen as the best way of carrying both troops and supplies, this role soon fell to transport aircraft, with the USAAC and Marine Corps switching from carrying priority personnel and cargo for deployed air units to inserting and supporting airborne forces. A militarised DC-3 was the best platform for carrying paratroopers or towing gliders into battle, although having been designed as an airliner, it was only an interim measure as a military transport.

Douglas designed two options – the C-47, which was a DC-3 with reinforced flooring and a large cargo door, and the C-53, which retained the smaller airline-style door. These aircraft, and camouflaged DC-3 airliners (primarily designated C-41s and C-48s through to C-52s, depending on equipment), were externally similar. R4Ds were simply Navy, Marine Corps or Coast Guard versions of the C-47.

Starting in 1941, in addition to C-47/R4Ds, production orders were also placed for more advanced military transport versions – with cargo

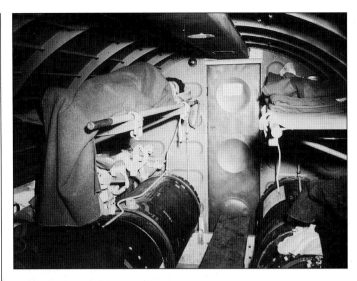

The cabin of a medical evacuation R4D, showing the older type (rigid support) stretchers and the 100-gallon auxiliary tanks that were in widespread use in both C-47s and R4Ds tasked with performing long-range flights in the Pacific (*National Archives*)

The first Marine Corps paratroopers board an R2D (a DC-2 with minimal modifications) at Quantico, in Virginia, in 1941. The Marine Corps had only embraced airborne forces for raiding and for integration with their amphibious mission that same year. This led to the adoption of the R4D for its 'utility' (later transport) units. While the Marine Corps formed regiment-sized paratroop units, and these made training jumps in the Pacific, they never went into battle that way. Rather than inserting paratroops from the air, R4Ds flew transport missions instead (*National Archives*)

doors and reinforced floors – of larger airliners including the twin-engined Curtiss C-46/R5C and the four-engined Douglas DC-4/R5D. But these all remained low-priority programmes, despite being ordered in big numbers, due to the desperate shortage of combat aircraft and trainers. Nevertheless, drawing boards were soon filled with designs for new transport aircraft, but it would be years before any would fly.

In 1941, there were few modern transport aircraft to support bases in Hawaii, the Philippines, Alaska and Panama, let alone land or sea combat in remote areas. The USAAC had no four-engined transports, and twin-engined land-based aircraft rarely ventured as far as Hawaii. Indeed, even within the USA, there was little more than a rudimentary network of bases for these aircraft to operate from. Pacific operations remained the domain of a few intrepid civilian pilots and a handful of large flying-boats. Planners, looking to create the forces needed for victory in Europe, simply ignored the air transport requirement of the coming Pacific War.

The US military did not learn the air transport lessons of the second Sino-Japanese War that raged in earnest from 1937. Once Japan had captured China's seaports, the latter's only remaining links with the outside world were airliners and the Burma Road. DC-2s and DC-3s of the Chinese National Airline Corporation (CNAC), owned jointly by the Chinese government and Pan American Airlines, and manned by veteran US and Chinese civilian crews, were in the frontline of the war, flying passengers and high-priority cargo. They were a vital element of Chinese air power when it came to resisting the Japanese, and the aircraft demonstrated tremendous reliability and ruggedness in harsh conditions.

For example, in 1941, a CNAC DC-3 that had had one of its wings destroyed in a Japanese air attack flew again with a replacement wing cannibalised from a DC-2. The new wing was five feet shorter, earning the aircraft immortality as the 'DC-2^{1}/$_{2}$'.

Ironically, the Japanese, who had been impressed by the efforts of the CNAC, bought manufacturing licences for three US airliners, with the intention of putting them into production as military transports – the Douglas DC-2, the Lockheed 14 and, finally, the Douglas DC-3.

The self-deployment of B-17 bombers to the Philippines in 1941 at last opened up a series of Pacific bases for land-based aircraft heading into the region from the USA. The

USAAC (US Army Air Force after June 1941) Ferry Command, which was formed in May 1941, was largely responsible for this. Primarily using contract airline crews at first, along with pilots recruited directly from civilian life, Ferry Command had the mission of delivering aircraft to US bases overseas, and, from October 1941, Lend-

Lease users. Routes to the Philippines, Alaska, Panama and Australia were created and new airfields built. Ferry Command started using flying-boats and converted bombers to reach Australia and the Philippines, as well as India (via the South Atlantic route, crossing Africa).

DC-3 types could fly from California to Hawaii with the aid of in-cabin ferry tanks, and the scarcity of larger transports meant that they also had to be used for transpacific services as well. Indeed, a Marine Corps R2D (DC-2) was the first aircraft to operate from the new runway on Midway Island, earning it the nickname *Gooney Bird* after the native long-winged albatross that lived on the island. This sobriquet soon became synonymous with all DC-2/3s the world over.

This early-production C-53 is seen here marked with pre-war white crosses as used during exercises in 1941. The USAAC had intended to send additional C-53s to the Philippines pre-war, these originally being scheduled to arrive in mid 1941. However, their shipment was delayed, and the five C-53s sent as deck cargo on merchant ships were diverted to Australia in early 1942 (*National Archives*)

TO WAR

The 7 December 1941 attack on Pearl Harbor destroyed Marine Corps R2Ds and damaged two USAAF C-33s of the 19th Transport Squadron (TS) and a Hawaiian Airlines DC-3. The twin-engined transport aircraft in the Philippines – a single C-39 and two converted B-18 bombers – survived the initial attacks, but were forced by Japanese air superiority in the region to leave Manila on the night of 17-18 December, arriving in Darwin, Australia, on 22 December.

The aircrew, and their passengers, had expected to fly back to the Philippines with bombers despatched from the USA, but following training by Australian airline crews, they were instead committed to combat with their aircraft, and five C-53s. The latter, despatched from California as deck cargo, had been diverted from the Philippines to Australia, where they had been hastily assembled.

The first missions carried out by the C-53s were to Java, with the aircraft flying in spare parts and groundcrew for the USAAF's P-40 units and evacuating wounded servicemen and civilians. On 28 January 1942, all available civil and military transport aircraft in Australia were formed

Again seen pre-war, this near-new C-39 was photographed at Mather Field, in California, in 1941. Performing both training and transport duties, most C-39s remained operational stateside until they were retired in 1944 (*Author's Collection*)

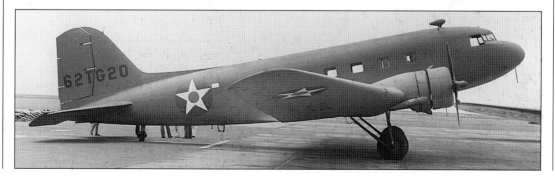

C-39 VH-CCF (marked up with an Australian civil registration) was among the first USAAF transport aircraft to arrive in Australia in 1942. Along with the one surviving C-39 from the Philippines, these machines served with the 21st and 22nd TCSs throughout the New Guinea campaign. This aircraft was eventually transferred to Australian National Airlines, and it crashed near Molesworth, Victoria, on 9 March 1944 (*National Archives*)

One of the first military C-47s to enter USAAF service was 41-7723, delivered in February 1942 and used by the ATC on transafrican routes. Having survived the war, and then served with the Minnesota Air National Guard into the 1960s, the aircraft was issued to the US Air Force Museum in 1971. The latter organisation in turn loaned it to the Pima Air and Space Museum in Tucson, Arizona, and the C-47 has been on display here for more than 35 years (*National Archives*)

into a joint Directorate of Air Transport (DAT). USAAF B-17 and B-24/LB-30 bombers – at the expense of their primary mission – also reinforced DAT. On 20 February, all US transport aircraft in Australia were formed into the 21st and 22nd TSs (redesignated Troop Carrier Squadrons in June).

By then, the Netherlands East Indies and Mindanao, in the Philippines, could only be reached by air, with flights being conducted at night due to the enemy's air superiority.

The last evacuation missions from Java were flown in the first week of March. DAT now had to prepare for the defence of Australia, re-supply New Guinea and evacuate areas threatened by the Japanese advance. Although the two USAAF squadrons shared just eight mechanics between them for eight weeks, they sustained a high operational tempo. For example, in March C-53 41-20070 flew 272 operational hours, reflecting the reliability and maintainability of these aircraft.

In the weeks after Pearl Harbor, the need for better communications with China led the USAAF to plan for 25 ex-airline DC-3s to deploy to India – it was thought that eventually as many as 75 transports might be required. The first to move out were ten Pan American Airways DC-3s with civilian crews, which followed the Ferry Command route, via Brazil, to India. Organised as the Assam-Burma-China Ferry Command in April 1942, they flew aviation gasoline from India to China to refuel Lt Col Jimmy Doolittle's B-25s, which planned to land near Chunking after their attack on Tokyo. Col William D Old flew the first India-China military flight on 8 April, carrying in fuel.

That same month, the 1st Ferrying Group – consisting of seven C-48s, 15 C-53s and three C-47s, with more coming – left Florida for Karachi, whilst four DC-3s, deployed from the Middle East, established the Trans-India Ferry Command. These aircraft, minus 12 diverted to the crisis in the Middle East, took part in the 22 April-15 June Allied air evacuation of Burma. The USAAF joined the RAF, Indian airliners and CNAC (veterans of the last flights out of Hong Kong and dozens of cities in China) in saving thousands, flying primarily from the pre-war RAF base at Myitkyina. One DC-3 carried out 74 passengers on a single flight.

Douglas transports carried out the evacuation with little logistics support, this improvised re-supply operation helping to save cut-off Chinese units and isolated British outposts. The USAAF, which delivered 870 tons of supplies and flew out 4500 personnel, lost several transports to ground strafing.

The Japanese advance soon severed both the overland and air routes (via Myitkyina) to China,

Early days on the 'Hump' in 1942-43. Chinese troops that are being redeployed by air read the 'blood chit' on the flying jacket of a pilot from one of the C-48s or early production C-53s that bore much of the burden of these initial airlifts in the CBI. Such individuals, and their aircraft, proved routes and established procedures that would be successfully refined in 1944-45 (*National Archives*)

causing the 'Flying Tigers' of the American Volunteer Group (AVG) to be grounded for lack of fuel in March-April 1942. Despite the loss of all Allied airfields in Burma, the US commitment to keep Chiang Kai-Shek's Chinese government in the war led to an airlift goal of 10,000 tons of supplies a month. The transportation of fuel and ammunition to the AVG in China became a priority, but overland supply routes that converged on Assam, in northern India, were at the end of a logistic shoestring stretching around the world. And the only way to penetrate the nearby Himalayas, and its neighbouring ranges (collectively known as the 'Hump'), and reach China from Assam was by air.

In April-May 1942, the newly-organised US Tenth Air Force combined with the CNAC to airlift 196 tons of supplies to China, although this figure fell to 85 tons in July. Improvisation kept aircraft flying, with R-1830-47 engines from Chinese P-43s being retrofitted to C-47s flying the 'Hump' so as to give them improved high altitude performance. Despite a Japanese bombing offensive against the airfields in Assam in October-November following the ending of the monsoon season, the modest supply tonnage figures began to increase, but the Tenth Air Force's tired aircraft were not accomplishing their mission.

In China, no aircraft could fly unless gasoline, ordnance and spares were first flown in from India, which itself stood vulnerable to the victorious Japanese. One aggressive C-47 crew attempted to take the war to the enemy during this period when it used a visit to the main 'Hump' terminal airfield of Kunming, in China, to make two unauthorised night bombing raids on Hanoi and Haiphong, rolling bombs out the cargo door. In 1942, American transport aircraft in the CBI had immense missions to fly with very few resources.

ATC AND NATS

In June 1942, Ferry Command – with 1000 aircraft and 11,000 personnel – was reorganised as Air Transport Command (ATC). The first truly global war-fighting organisation, ATC was directly under the command of USAAF Headquarters in Washington, DC. This meant that local commanders could only use ATC transports, aircrew or cargo in dire emergencies. ATC's five organisational – not operational – wings

The *"CHASTITY CHARIOT"* was probably the first C-47 to serve with the USAAF in the CBI, having originally been an RAF Dakota I. Its large cargo door was a tremendous innovation for aircraft servicing China, the C-47 being able to airlift Allison engines for the 'Flying Tigers'. Serving with the 1st Ferry Group and flying the 'Hump' from 1942 until at least early 1943, the aircraft was painted in RAF camouflage, but had had its roundels poorly overpainted with 1942-period national markings. Amongst its many pilots during that time were (from left to right) Lts Jack 'Mac' McReynolds, Richard J Taylor and H W Gesner (*National Archives*)

This DC-3A, which was impressed into ATC service as a C-53 on 18 January 1942, displays the early versions of the national roundel and ATC insignia. Local personnel – here in their dress uniforms for the benefit of the photographer – demonstrate how the absence of a cargo door limited the utility of these aircraft, even with low-weight cargo. The ATC relied as much as possible on locally recruited personnel to load and unload aircraft, many of whom soon became highly proficient at this important task. This particular aircraft (41-20080) operated on transafrican communication routes to the CBI until withdrawn in April 1944 and scrapped (*National Archives*)

(eventually to become divisions) covered the world. The domestic wing flew priority missions and, increasingly, trained crews for long-range operations, the Africa-Middle East Wing crossed Africa and the Middle East, and the South Pacific Wing flew DC-3s to Australia, via Palmyra and Canton Islands, Fiji and New Caledonia.

As with an airline, ATC crews and transports did not normally belong to a specific squadron (with some exceptions, especially in the CBI in 1942-43). C-47s used the newly opened route from Hawaii to New Zealand through Christmas Island, Bora Bora, Aitukaki Island and Tonga. These remote island fields became part of the Allied lifeline to the emerging South Pacific and South West Pacific theatres.

The Naval Air Transport Service (NATS), organised in December 1941 to provide worldwide transport support for the US Navy, reflected the lessons of 1940-41 operations by demonstrating the importance of air transport in keeping warships and shore-based aviation units forward deployed. NATS made extensive use of R4Ds, despite their range limitations, to bring priority cargo and personnel forward to their ships and aircraft operating across the globe.

A typical NATS R4D load – a spare engine, priority cargo and life-rafts. Flying spare engines was difficult for bombers, PBYs and other dedicated military aircraft pressed into service as transports. The ability to have spare engines flown to forward airstrips by C-47s and R4Ds (which would then take away engines needing repair) was as important to the use of air power in the Pacific and CBI as the ability of engineers and Seabees to build airstrips from which these aircraft could take the fight to the enemy (*National Archives*)

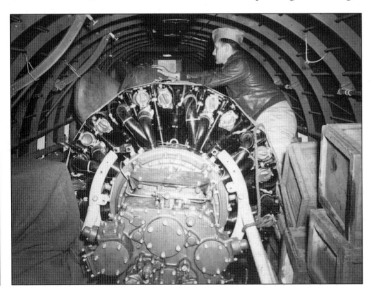

DECISIVE BATTLES

Days after Pearl Harbor, commandeered DC-3s flew troops to Hawaiian islands thought threatened by invasion. Hawaii-based transports airlifted munitions to Midway Island and evacuated wounded and downed aircrew. Even before the Japanese invasion of Attu and Kiska in June 1942, DC-3s were critical to communications in the vast state of Alaska. Northwest Airlines had flown a survey flight of the region in February, and it was soon servicing the route from Great Falls, Montana, to Fairbanks under contract,

C-53-DO 41-20073 *Butchie 2* of the Seventh Air Force's 19th TS returns to Hawaii from NAS Midway on 8 June 1942. Capt Stephen J Rosetta was at the controls on this flight, the ex-airline pilot going on to command the redesignated 19th TCS in 1943-44. The crowd around the aeroplane includes news-starved reporters, desperate to find out about the recently fought Battle of Midway. The C-53 has national insignia in six-positions, which was a US Navy-imposed requirement for aircraft operating between Hawaii and Midway at that time. The widespread application of 'new' olive drab paint suggests that pre-war upper-wing unit identification has been painted out (*National Archives*)

In 1942, it was thought that C-47Cs on floats would be just what was needed in the Pacific. More than 100 sets of floats were built by Edo at its College Point, New York, factory, but by the time they were ready, it had been demonstrated that land-based aircraft, using runways hastily built by engineers, were the solution. A few C-47Cs were used operationally in 1944-45, including one in the Aleutians, another in New Guinea and the Philippines, and one in the CBI (based near Calcutta) (*National Archives*)

being joined by Western and United Airlines. USAAF C-47s flew the first medical evacuation missions from Alaska in January 1942.

US forces relied heavily on air transport to sustain aircraft operations from remote forward airfields in the Aleutians, with these supply missions often being flown in marginal weather conditions that in peacetime would have been considered prohibitive. ATC Alaskan Wing was activated in October 1942, with NATS providing support.

In the South Pacific, Guadalcanal, invaded by Allied forces in August 1942, urgently needed air transport due to Japanese air and naval strength preventing convoys from resupplying the island stronghold. Thirteen Marine Corps R4D-1s (each with eight 100 gallon ferry tanks in the cabin) of VMJ-253 duly flew from San Diego to Ewa, in Hawaii, on 23 August and deployed via the southern air route to New Caledonia. This squadron, like its USAAF counterparts, was manned by a cadre of former airline pilots with skills – including radio navigation – that were to be particularly valuable during the coming campaign.

On 3 September, just 14 days after the first US fighters landed on Guadalcanal, an R4D flew the first airlift into the embattled island's

Henderson Field, carrying in the commanding officer of the 1st Marine Air Wing, Brig Gen Roy Geiger, and his staff. The subsequent airlift operated from New Caledonia via a forward base at Espiritu Santo, flying in ammunition, personnel, gasoline and other priority cargo, and evacuating wounded troops. Air operations from Henderson Field were dependent on the airlift, and nocturnal flights continued even when transports could no longer remain on the ground in daylight for fear of being shot at. Each load of 12-15 aviation fuel barrels flown in per C-47/R4D meant that a fighter could fly for an hour in defence of Guadalcanal.

When reinforcement fighters arrived, they relied on transports to act as their pathfinders, as the flight from Espiritu Santo was an 880-mile trek over water, the last hour of which was within range of Japanese fighters.

R4D-equipped VMJ-152, which was also part of Marine Air Group (MAG) 25, arrived in-theatre in October, as did the 13 C-47s of the USAAF's 13th TCS. Boosting the force in the South Pacific Area were seven C-47s of the 33rd TCS, which were diverted from their ferry mission to Australia as they passed through the area in October-November and committed to the Guadalcanal airlift for a month – total transport strength now numbered 50 aircraft. The C-47s and R4Ds were quickly organised into the joint service South Pacific Combat Air Transport Command (SCAT), which provided a single in-theatre airlift manager.

At the height of the campaign, between 12 and 14 October, SCAT sent eight transports per night into Henderson laden with fuel. That month alone, 105 tons of cargo, five tons of mail and 339 personnel were successfully airlifted into Guadalcanal. C-47s, supplemented

A Marine Corps R4D of SCAT is worked on by TSgts Eldon Dennis and Frank Geist. The position of the aircraft number '82' on the engine nacelle rather than the cowling was a common practice amongst Marine Corps R4D units. Most of the C-47 and R4D squadrons deploying to the South Pacific in 1942 had to send their ground echelons by sea, and it was often several months before they arrived and had their equipment unloaded (*National Archives*)

R4D '1' of VMJ-253 prepares to be unloaded at Henderson Field, on Guadalcanal, in February 1943. The officer walking towards the camera is Gen Russell E Rowell, USMC, CO of the Marine Corps' Pacific Air Wings. This aircraft was one of the first 13 Marine Corps R4Ds sent to the South Pacific, where they proved vital in re-supplying Guadalcanal in 1942-43. Like most Marine Corps R4Ds, they were painted in olive drab/neutral grey, with a one or two-digit aircraft number (and no visible serial) to identify it. This aircraft had also been used to fly Brig Gen Roy Geiger in to take command of all aviation units at Henderson Field in September 1942 (*National Archives*)

R4D '27' of the Marine Corps makes its final approach to Henderson Field in early 1943. This aircraft's identification number appears in black on the forward cargo door (*National Archives*)

by bombers, also airdropped supplies to Marine Corps 'Raider' patrols outside the main defensive perimeter. From September to December 1942, transports evacuated 2900+ casualties – nearly three times as many as were evacuated by ship. A VMJ-253 report described the operations;

'Take-off was usually made as soon as the aeroplane was fuelled and loaded – usually about 0100 hrs – and it then headed north towards the Solomons. The flight was made just beneath the low lying clouds, where the visibility was good and the pilot ducked into a cloud bank and flew on instruments whenever anything suspicious was sighted. Upon reaching San Cristobal, the standard practice was to let down to 50 or 75 ft and continue on to Henderson Field.'

2Lt Robert Sexton of the 13th TCS made his first flight into Henderson Field on 23 October;

'They didn't have the holes in the runway filled when we landed. Flights to the Solomons were strenuous as hell. We'd try to hit the islands at dawn, so we had to fly at night – the worst time. Once we'd reached the field at Guadalcanal, we had to immediately taxi to one end of the strip. A Japanese field piece we called "Pistol Pete" had just enough range to hit the near end, so we'd land and then run like hell for the other end where we wouldn't get shot up. The squadron flew supplies in and wounded out. One of our aircraft landed one morning just as three Japanese ship transports full of Nips came in. It was sort of messy for a while.'

Most maintenance was carried out by the aircrew themselves, along with one or two groundcrew per aircraft that had travelled into Henderson with the C-47/R4D. As for equipment, MTSgt J D Huggins of VMJ-253 recalled, 'We had the kit of hand tools that came with the aeroplane', and that was it. The Marines Corps' ground echelon did not arrive until October, yet despite this, serviceability was high. For example, the 13th TCS had only three in-flight C-47 engine failures in four-and-a-half years of operations, and two of them were experi-

Capt C Campbell (an ex-airline pilot and veteran of the Guadalcanal airlift) and MSgt Luther Inge (right) are seen at the controls of ~~an R4D of VMJ-253~~ in 1943 (*National Archives*) B-24 / PB4Y ?

enced by the same C-47 (41-18590) coming back – fully loaded – from Guadalcanal. On both occasions, the same right engine kept turning until the aircraft reached Espiritu Santo, 105 minutes flying time away.

Japanese aircraft were only encountered, and evaded, on several missions, as US transport tactics minimised contact with enemy fighters. 1Lt Eben Hinton of the 13th TCS was approaching Guadalcanal, under an overcast, when a Zero dived through it. It immediately climbed back into the overcast. Within seconds, it reappeared, in a spin, and crashed into the ocean. Hinton learned at Henderson that he had flown under a dogfight. In another incident, fighters shot down a Japanese aircraft that attacked a transport after it had taken off. Finally, SSgt Ray Hensman's C-47 41-38628 *Pack Rat* of the 33rd TCS was downed by enemy flak off the northern end of Henderson Field on 8 November.

A 13th TCS C-47 approaches Henderson Field in 1943, this aircraft having been used in the Guadalcanal airlift in September-November 1942. One of the locally-based J2F Ducks, used for utility and rescue missions, is holding at the end of the runway waiting for the C-47 to land (*National Archives*)

Other R4Ds and C-47s linked the forward bases in the New Hebrides and New Caledonia to Hawaii, Australia and New Zealand. The inadequate port facilities and consequent shipping backlogs at many of these forward bases placed additional importance on ATC's routes from Hawaii to New Caledonia (where SCAT took over). In January, 1943 the USAAF's 801st Medical Air Evacuation Squadron took over casualty evacuation missions from Guadalcanal on SCAT aircraft, bringing with it the first specialist flight nurses to reach the South Pacific. Mobile base units also began appearing throughout the theatre, allowing air operations from newly opened airstrips.

NEW GUINEA 1942-43

The Japanese invaded New Guinea on 21 July 1942, seizing the airfields at Lae, Salamaua and Buna and launching an offensive – accompanied by repeated air attacks – on the capital of Port Moresby and its vital airfields. They also advanced across the fearsome Owen Stanley Range, which boasted peaks up to 8000 ft high that were covered with dense rain forest and separated by deep ravines and interlacing gorges. Roads were non-existent in-country, and the Japanese quickly showed their skill in jungle warfare by dislodging air-supplied Australian forces from the critical mission station at Kokoda on 9 August.

Changes in command enabled an effective Allied response to the crisis, however. Maj Gen George Kenney became commander of the Fifth Air Force and Allied Air Forces, South West Pacific Area (SWPA), directly subordinate to Gen Douglas MacArthur, the overall theatre commander-in-chief, on 4 August 1942. Kenney saw that the transports, no less than bombers and fighters, were vital to success in New Guinea, and MacArthur's command allowed Allied forces to be effectively integrated.

The few Australian and US air and ground forces in New Guinea were dependent on DAT, including 32 US transports and a few converted bombers, flying from Brisbane to airstrips outside of Port Moresby – 1400 miles, over water, for aircraft that had been without overhaul or repair for many months. Other DAT transports based at Port Moresby supplied frontline troops. DAT crews, both US and Australian, were soon working with the troops, improvising parachute re-supply and medical evacuations. Neither training nor pre-war doctrine provided guidance.

The pattern was soon set – many small, often single-aeroplane, missions from Port Moresby to forward strips or to airdrop supplies.

This US Army theatre map released in 1945 reveals the vast area covered by C-47 transports in the SWPA. The black arrows mark the various Allied offensives that eventually resulted in the defeat of Japanese forces in the region (*US Army*)

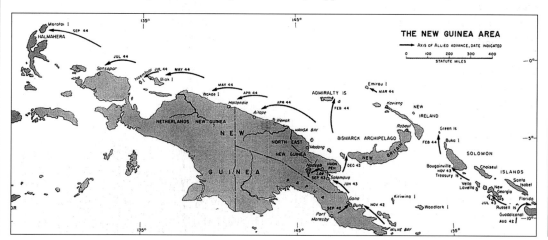

17

C-47 pilot Capt William Embry of the 41st TCS, who was interviewed in 1942, described the weather in which crews flew from Port Moresby;

'Sometimes we can get through certain passes at 9000 ft before the weather builds up – and it really builds up, about noon. I guess some of the highest thunderheads in the world are in this region. On the other hand, if we have to fly on instruments and give ourselves a safe margin of clearance, we sometimes have to fly as high as 17,000 ft. That's darned high for a loaded C-47. We have also had to fly around the southern tip of New Guinea to get back to Port Moresby in the late afternoon.'

The airlift had to split the few transports available between supporting the troops in the field, supporting the air forces and airlifting needed reinforcements and supplies from Australia. Extra C-47s were delayed by the Guadalcanal campaign, leaving DAT with just 78 transports in September – 41 (15 non-flyable) of them USAAF – to both supply the troops and fly in reinforcements.

Although air attacks on Port Moresby destroyed transports, they did not halt the airlifts. One C-47, hit on the ground and almost cut in half, had its control cables re-connected by 'splintering' them with lumber to allow the transport to be flown back to Australia by Capt 'Pappy' Gunn, the Fifth Air Force's indefatigable ordnance chief, for repairs.

TSgt Lee Grace was one of the groundcrew sustaining the high pace of operations with minimal resources;

'A ten-hour inspection ought to involve eight men, four on each engine. In those days, we had just five men, with one crew helping another. It took all night for that number of men to do the job, but air raids would slow us up. We'd have to douse the lights and run for a slit trench. Then it took us a little longer.'

Air re-supply sustained Australian forces holding the Kokoda Trail and Milne Bay. Soon, 25 tons a day were airdropped by DAT, about half of which was recovered. Even hard-pressed B-26s were diverted to airdrop missions. At first, crews would try and drop as much as possible in each pass over the drop zone (DZ). Soon, however, they learned that precision was more important than volume, so they made up to ten passes. Not all cargo required scarce parachutes, and as an expedient, food, if securely wrapped, could make do with just streamers to help mark its location.

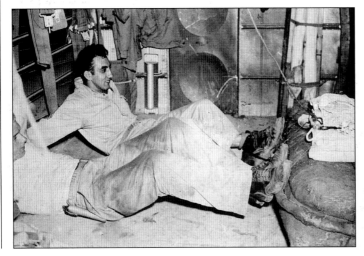

Vital to the C-47's mission in New Guinea were the 'pushers' and 'kickers', who were normally volunteer ground personnel that, assisted by aircrew, would get cargo – here with a parachute attached – out of the main door over the DZ. While the use of internal cargo handling equipment increased, the need for a quick response to hit small DZs meant that most of this procedure remained manual to the end of the war in the Pacific and CBI (*National Archives*)

Troops also became more proficient at selecting DZs and marking them with smoke and panels.

Airlifts from Australia brought up reinforcements, and in September, these troops counterattacked. Three battalions of Australian soldiers flown into Port Moresby, and supported by airdrops, pushed back the Japanese, weakened by an unsustainable logistics trail. Additional airlifts of troops – increasing the force's size until full Australian and US divisions had arrived – sustained the offensive. In addition to air re-supply (100+ tons brought in daily to New Guinea), the campaign depended on troop airlift, both from Australia to Port Moresby and from there to forward airstrips, starting when Kokoda was recaptured on 2 November.

Ground forces quickly leapfrogged forward by airlift to fields identified by reconnaissance, with forward strips such as that at Wangela being increasingly used from September, when a detachment of Australian engineers hacked it out of the vegetation. Once the strip was declared open, over the coming hours 12 C-47s (with P-39 escorts) carrying 3600 troops were flown in during the course of 71 sorties. The advance on Buna, codenamed Operation *Hatrack*, required the airlift of 10,000+ personnel to forward airstrips, and the evacuation of the wounded. DAT had 20 transports – ten of them Douglas twins – primarily for evacuation, and they flew out more than 13,000 casualties during the campaign.

While individual C-47s had been arriving in Australia since the spring, and were allocated as replacement aircraft, the first squadron completely equipped with the type (the 6th TCS) arrived in Australia in mid-October, followed in October-November by the 33rd, which was diverted to Guadalcanal. The 374th TCG HQ was activated under DAT in November to control the four TCSs operational in the Fifth Air Force.

Although USAAF doctrine focused on airborne assault, troop carrier units readily adapted to the transport missions required in-theatre. The improvisation of an effective ground infrastructure made quick turn-arounds possible, thanks to US air freight forwarding units, DAT's cargo regulating officers (to set and implement priorities) and experienced Allied troops and Papuans physically loading and unloading aircraft.

Most of the missions were flown in daylight, usually without escorts, despite aggressive Japanese fighters and anti-aircraft fire. The C-47's manoeuvrability often meant safety through evasive action or diving for cloud cover, but those caught taking off or landing were often shot down. Two C-47s were lost to fighters in this way in November alone. Losses were so high – both to enemy action and operational causes – that Maj Gen Kenney told Washington 'a man lives longer in a P-39 than in a C-47'. Transport crews were averaging 100 hours a month, and Kenney wanted to send them home after 500 hours, but a shortage of replacement crews kept them in action for much longer.

The liberation of Buna (23 January 1943) closed the 1942 New Guinea campaign. Air transport had enabled Allied ground forces to beat the Japanese in jungle warfare where they had previously been all-conquering. MacArthur understood that transports did not just move

C-47-DL 41-38665 of the 6th TCS taxies in at Port Moresby after flying troops of the US 32nd Infantry Division back from Dobodura on 4 February 1943. USAAF and RAAF transports were used interchangeably for many missions under DAT. This aircraft, which arrived in Australia with the 317th TCG in January 1943, operated with the Fifth Air Force throughout the war (*National Archives*)

and supply ground forces, they shaped strategy. He commented, 'The railroad car of the last war has been replaced by the C-47 aeroplane. Men, food, munitions and artillery now go by air. War as waged in New Guinea would be impossible without air transportation'.

This campaign, like the one fought at Guadalcanal, set a pattern for Allied success. As with amphibious operations, the objective became to advance where the Japanese were weak, bypassing garrisons wherever possible. Transport aircraft would drop supplies to the frontline, evacuate wounded and fly in reinforcements. Ground forces would fight to secure airfields for land-based air power, which would make possible further advances. Engineers, whether airlifted or amphibious, built airfields and infrastructure, USAAF engineer units and Navy Construction Battalions ('Seabees') being expert in rapid airfield construction.

While the vast majority of cargo and personnel were still moved by sea, air transportation proved decisive. Indeed, troops at the 'sharp end' were now increasingly supplied and medically evacuated by air.

NEW GUINEA 1943

The first complete Troop Carrier Group to deploy to the SWPA from the US was the 317th TCG, its 52 C-47s arriving in Australia just in time to be committed to an emergency airlift into the beleaguered airhead at Wau. Starting on 29 January, the C-47s flew 2000 troops into Wau in just 48 hours, aircraft manoeuvring down a valley between fog-shrouded mountains and landing on a 3000-ft strip built on a 12 per cent slope. C-47s often had to circle the field until Australian counterattacks could clear the Japanese away from its perimeter. Escorted C-47s fought their way through enemy fighters and survived bomber attacks on the airstrip.

Landing and unloading was also done under fire, and 11 C-47s were lost (five eventually rebuilt) at Wau, which now became a base for the advance on Lae, sustaining a 300-ton a day airlift in March-April.

The 317th shared the near-universal appreciation of the C-47's qualities for New Guinea. Capt William Embry of the 41st TCS recalled;

'All of us think the Douglas C-47 is about the best type of ship in the world for the type of work we do. With any other aeroplane, we certainly couldn't land on these muddy, short fields with loads of between 5000 and 6000 lbs. When you try and land that load on a 2000-ft strip, you have to know your aeroplane is good – and we know that.'

In February, the 317th left its new C-47s behind in New Guinea for the veteran 374th TCG and took the latter group's war-weary collection of transports that it had been flying throughout 1942 back to Australia. The 317th operated these aircraft under DAT control until replacement C-47s arrived.

Maj Gen Kenney had been promised four Troop Carrier Groups for the 1943 campaign. To command

This war-weary C-47 of the 375th TCG is about to evacuate wounded Australian troops to Port Moresby from northern New Guinea in late 1943 (*TSgt Walter D Kudler via Author's Collection*)

them, the 54th Troop Carrier Wing (TCW), under Col (later Brig Gen) Paul Prentiss, was activated. Yet despite production increases, the Fifth Air Force had to fight for C-47s and crews, competing with the impending invasion of Sicily and the need to form and train Troop Carrier Groups stateside for the 1944 invasion of Europe. In 1943, aircrew and aircraft were kept in action in New Guinea long after they would have been retired in other theatres. By September, there were 14 Troop Carrier Squadrons (each supposedly equipped with 13 aircraft) in the Fifth Air Force, all fully committed to transport missions.

In 1942, to support the campaign, ATC had expanded its services to Australia. However, Washington barred ATC from flying directly to New Guinea, which in turn meant that the delivery of priority cargo some 1500 miles from where it was needed proved to be of limited value. Weary DAT crews duly had to carry these cargoes from Australia to New Guinea in barely serviceable C-47s, while the ATC went back to the US for another load. The bitter Fifth Air Force jibe that ATC meant 'Allergic To Combat' endured even when that problem was resolved.

As ATC gained enough personnel to regularly operate the routes to Australia, it renamed its South Pacific Wing the West Coast Wing in December 1942, forming a new Pacific Wing, headquartered at Hickam Field, in January 1943. That same month, ATC had 350 twin- and four-engined transports on strength, 250 of them being C-47/DC-3 types. By June 1943, ATC was flying critical aircraft parts – and parachutes for coming airborne assaults – directly to Port Moresby. Further alleviating the Fifth Air Force's transport burden, ATC commenced an intratheatre service in July, with five C-47s linking Port Moresby with Australia.

Infrastructure improvements made transport aircraft more effective in the 1943 campaign. Improved support facilities in Australia and at Port Moresby kept C-47s in action longer thanks to increased serviceability. A new DAT terminal at Milne Bay allowed quicker unloading of aircraft and transfer of equipment to end-users, and improved airdrop techniques led to 85-90 per cent of supplies being recovered.

The Allied offensive against Lae required an intermediate air base, so the old airstrip at Tsili Tsili was secured and C-47s flew in a company of USAAF airborne engineers with miniature bulldozers. Despite bad weather, and Japanese fighters that shot down the first two C-47s to arrive, the first US fighters flew in on 15 July, and within three weeks Tsili Tsili was receiving 150 transports a day thanks to improved ground cargo handling techniques. At nearby Marilinan, trucks and construction equipment were cut in half to fit into C-47s and welded together on arrival, allowing a new airfield to be built. Pre-fabricated pierced steel planking for runways was brought in aboard C-47s, some of which were flown by Capt George Kutche, operations officer of the 41st TCS;

'We once flew in a 5000-ft runway. It was broken into about 90 pieces per aeroplane, and it took lots of C-47s to bring it in. It was a maximum load under those conditions. These runways are necessary for the fighters, which cannot land under the rough conditions that we can. The strip we were flying off actually had loose gravel on it, and I tore up a dozen aeroplane tyres in those few days.'

To help conclude the Lae campaign, on 5 September, the US Army's 503rd Parachute Infantry Regiment (PIR), reinforced by Australian

A formation of C-47s flies over New Guinea with a P-40 escort (tucked in beneath the centre aircraft) in July 1943. The escort's altitude suggests that they were primarily tasked with suppressing any anti-aircraft weapons that opened fire during the airdrop, rather than defending the transports from Japanese fighters (*National Archives*)

Gen Douglas MacArthur, commander-in-chief of the South West Pacific Area, and Maj Gen George Kenney, commander of the Fifth Air Force (in flight jacket at right) discuss the impending Nadzab airdrop with Col George M Jones, commanding officer of the 503rd PIR, shortly before take-off on 5 September 1943 (*National Archives*)

artillery, made the first parachute assault of the Pacific War at Nadzab airfield, 30 miles inland from the site of the amphibious invasion of Lae made the previous day. Some 1700 troops were lifted by 79 C-47s of the 54th TCW, led personally by Prentiss, from Port Moresby, over the Owen Stanleys, to Nadzab – a distance of 200+ miles. Coordinated with fighter and bomber attacks, it was a complete success, including the parachute drop of disassembled artillery – the first time this had been attempted in combat.

The parachute assault attracted high level interest, with Gen MacArthur and Maj Gen Kenney observing. The latter described what he saw to USAAF chief of staff, Gen Henry 'Hap' Arnold;

'I will tell you about the show on 5 September, when we took Nadzab with 1700 paratroops, and with Gen MacArthur in a B-17 over the area watching the show and jumping up and down like a kid. I was flying No 2 in the same flight with him, and the operation really was a magnificent spectacle. I truly don't believe that another air force in the world today could have put this over as perfectly as the Fifth did. Some 320 aeroplanes in all, taking off from eight different fields in the Moresby and Dobodura areas, made a rendezvous right on the nose over Marilinan, flying through clouds, passes in mountains and over the top.

'Not a single squadron circled or stalled around, but all slid into place like clockwork and proceeded on the final flight down the Watut Valley, turned to the right down the Markham and then directly to the target.

'Going north down Watut Valley from Marilinan, this was the picture – heading the parade at 1000 ft were six squadrons of B-25 strafers, with eight 0.50-cal guns in the nose and 60 frag bombs in each bomb-bay. Immediately behind, and 500 ft above, were six A-20s flying in pairs (three pairs abreast), laying smoke as the last frag bomb exploded.

'At about 2000 ft, and directly behind the A-20s, came 96 C-47s carrying paratroops, supplies, and some artillery. The C-47s flew in three columns of three-aeroplane elements, each column carrying a battalion set up for a particular battalion dropping ground. On each side along the column of transports and 1000 ft above them were the close-cover fighters. Another group of fighters sat at 7000 ft and, up in the sun, staggered from 15,000 ft to 20,000 ft, was still another group.

This photograph was taken during the paratroop assault on Nadzab on 5 September 1943. The C-47s dropping paratroops are flying through the smoke screen put down by low-flying A-20s (*National Archives*)

A follow-up supply drop was made for paratroops in the Markham Valley on 6 September 1943, the broad open valley allowing the C-47s to deliver supplies in the preferred vee formation. In the smaller drop zones more typical of New Guinea, aircraft would have to drop singly, making repeated passes (*National Archives*)

'Following the transports came five B-17s, racks loaded with 300-lb packages with parachutes, to be dropped to the paratroopers on call by panel signals as they needed them. This mobile supply unit stayed over Nadzab all day serving the paratroops, dropping 15 tons of supplies.

'Following the echelon to the right and just behind the five supply B-17s was a group of 24 B-24s and four B-17s, which left the column just before the junction of the Watut and the Markham to take out the defensive position at Heath's Plantation, between Nadzab and Lae. Five weather ships were used prior to and during the show along the route and over the passes to keep the units straight on weather to be encountered during their flights to the rendezvous. The "brass-hat" flight of three B-17s above the centre of the transport column completed the set-up.

'The strafers checked in on the target at exactly the time set, just prior to take-off. They strafed and frag-bombed the whole area in which the jumps were to be made, and then as the last bombs exploded the smoke layers went to work. As the streams of smoke were built up, three columns of C-47s slid into place, and in one minute and ten seconds from the time the first parachute opened, the last of 1700 paratroopers had dropped.'

Following Col Prentiss in the lead C-47 *The Honeymoon Express* was Maj Herbert Waldman, commanding officer of the 41st TCS. He was leading the third three-ship vee of the formation;

'We all had the exact location in our minds – it was in the Markham Valley, just 25 miles from Lae. Our objective was to seal the backdoor to Lae. And this we did, and captured it nine days later. It is now one of our most important bases in the forward areas.

'We were held up before taking off, waiting for favourable weather reports and the time that had been set as the zero hour. Then, on a visual signal, we started up and taxied around in order to take off. The ship I was flying was number seven to take off and, in order to make the formation, it was necessary after taking off to fly straight ahead for 30 miles so that all ships could get off the ground and turn into position with us. We then proceeded on course – we led the entire formation.'

No transport aircraft were lost and 95 percent of the personnel hit their drop zones, where they encountered minimal resistance. The parachute

C-47A-35-DL 42-23880 *SURE SKIN*, of the 68th TCS/433rd TCG carried this artwork during its time in New Guinea in 1943-44 (*Author's Collection*)

C-47A-35-DL 42-23880 *SURE SKIN* of the 68th TCS/433rd TCG was the first Allied aeroplane to land at Lae-Finschhafen, in New Guinea, on 18 December 1943 when it led in a large formation of transports. Here photographed over the Owen Stanleys, note that the aircraft's national insignia – in this case the 1943 red-bordered version – has, in common with many aircraft in the Pacific, had the red fade out of it. As seen on page 23, the C-47 had a pin-up on the port side under the cockpit. Note also the mission scoreboard (relatively rare in New Guinea because of the number of missions flown) aft of the cockpit. C-47 crews were specifically asked not to publicise the number of combat missions they flew so as to avoid tension with Eighth Air Force veterans stateside! This aircraft was transferred to ATC in 1944, and post-war it operated as an airliner in Chile until retired in the 1970s (*National Archives*)

assault and subsequent supply airdrops, coordinated with fighter and bomber attacks, were a success. Nadzab airfield proved to be in good enough shape that a lift of 11 CG-4A gliders with engineering equipment was cancelled in favour of having C-47s fly directly into the base.

Starting on 6 September, the Australian 7th Division was flown into Nadzab from Tsili Tsili, where it had been previously airlifted. Some 420 aeroplane-loads of infantry arrived over five days. Nadzab continued to be re-supplied by air (200 sorties per day) until December, when a road was completed from Lae.

Transport aircraft – assisted by bombers pressed into a transport role – made possible the forward advance of Allied air power in New Guinea. C-47s had propelled Allied units from their bases around Port Moresby to new ones in the north, which in turn made possible multiple advances in the region. Support of ground operations also included large numbers of airdrop and medical evacuation missions. In 1943 alone, some 52,000+ casualties were evacuated by air in the SWPA.

433rd TCG C-47s participate in the big daylight fly-in of fighter unit groundcrews and supplies to Lae-Finschhafen airstrip on 18 December 1943 (*National Archives*)

Flight nurse 2Lt Elizabeth Dodd (armed with a standard 0.45-cal pistol and wearing a Fifth Air Force shoulder insignia) checks the list of wounded to be evacuated, and their required in-flight medical care, at Hollandia in early 1944 (*National Archives*)

CBI 1942-44

At the end of 1942, with the Japanese no longer poised to launch a major offensive against India from Burma, and Allied counterattacks delayed by the theatre's low priority in resources, the focus of air transport in the CBI theatre became the airlift to China over the 'Hump'. In December 1942, ATC took over the air re-supply mission to China from the Tenth Air Force, establishing its India-China Wing as controlling headquarters. This made the 'Hump' airlift independent of the campaign against the Japanese in Burma, thus reflecting the US government's top-level strategic priority – not shared by the British – of keeping China in the war. It also added to the confused command relationships that hamstrung air power in the CBI.

In mid 1942, the cargo to China objective was reset to a more achievable 4000 tons per month, although ATC still found it hard to ramp up to this level. Aircrew, aircraft and infrastructure alike were all lacking. Bases in Assam were difficult to reach by road from Indian ports, and these roads were often inoperable in the monsoon season. Aircraft serviceability was also poor, whilst ATC crews lacked training for mountain flying. 'Hump' routes generally ran for 720 miles, and required C-47s to fly at an altitude of at least 20,000 ft, especially after Japanese fighters closed off the lower altitude routes over northern Burma.

The high-altitude route soon became known as the 'Aluminium Highway', as it was paved with crashed aircraft. Surviving a tour of duty (initially 750 hours, but later reduced to 650) often seemed impossible. More lethal than the Japanese were unexpected weather changes, equipment failure and navigation errors over uncharted mountains. One lost crew made repeated radio calls for position fixes. Then, after a last call, singing loudly in the grips of lethal hypoxia (oxygen failure), they vanished among the peaks.

With navigation aids scarce, crews quickly learned to descend through overcasts in narrow mountain valleys by spiralling down around a radio beacon in a 60-degree bank. Kunming, in a valley, and liable to be socked in for extended periods, was one of the first 'Hump' fields to receive

Heading out on a mission from the airfield in Sookerating, Assam, in July 1943, the closest aircraft in this photograph was one of the first USAAF C-47s built, whilst the middle transport was a converted DC-3 (probably a C-48). As can clearly be seen, the surface over which these aircraft are taxiing would easily become a sea of mud in rainy conditions. All three transports are part of the 13th Ferry Squadron/1st Ferry Group (*National Archives*)

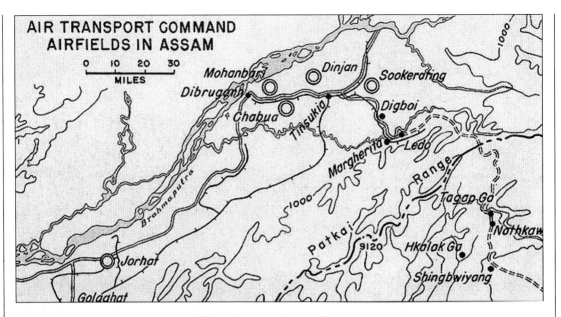

AIR TRANSPORT COMMAND
AIRFIELDS IN ASSAM

0   10   20   30
MILES

Mohanbari   Dinjan   Sookerating
Dibrugarh
Chabua   Tinsukia   Digboi
Margherita   Ledo
Brahmaputra   Range   Tagap Ga
1000   Nathkaw
Patkai   9120   Hkalak Ga
Jorhat   Shingbwiyang
Golaghat

proper terminal control. Brig Gen William Tunner, who was later to command the 'Hump' effort, described prevailing weather conditions;

'In these clouds, over the entire route, turbulence would build up of a severity greater than I have ever seen anywhere else in the world, before or since. Winds of as much as 100 mph piling into the steep barren slopes would glance off to create updrafts over the ridges and downdrafts over the valleys. Aeroplanes caught in a downdraft could drop at the rate of 5000 ft per minute, then suddenly be whisked upwards at almost the same speed. These tremendous storms would come on with great suddenness – there was no way to telling the amount of turbulence within a cloud until you were in it.

'The worst storm we ever had on the "Hump" occurred earlier than the usual spring thunderstorms, in January, but its characteristics were the same. It brought violent gusts and updrafts, along with severe icing, sleet and hail. A 100-mph wind, howling across our east-west routes directly from the south, blew aeroplanes far to the north among the high Himalayas. Conditions were the same from 15,000 ft up to 38,000 ft – we couldn't get under and we couldn't get over.'

Despite all these obstacles, the tonnage started to rise. In June, ATC had 146 transports committed to the 'Hump' and delivered 2219 tons to China, while CNAC, with 20 DC-3s, delivered 761 tons. In September, ATC, now with 225 transports, delivered 5198 tons, while CNAC, with 23 DC-3s, delivered 1134 tons. ATC's goal was to replace all C-47s flying the 'Hump' with larger, more powerful C-46s, but the first of these to reach the CBI proved to be so unreliable that they were returned to the US for repairs. ATC would have to rely on C-47s well into 1944.

In December 1942, the Tenth Air Force had only eight USAAF C-47/53s – war-weary returnees from the Middle East – to support operations in India and Burma, whilst the China Air Task Force (later to become the Fourteenth Air Force) had just a single C-47. Lack of air re-supply subsequently led to the failure of the first Allied ground offensive in Burma, in the Arakan, in December 1942.

This wartime map reveals the location of ATC airfields in India's northeastern state of Assam (*US Army*)

Marked, appropriately, with a '1' on its nose, this C-47 was the first of its type based in China (at Kweilin) with the USAAF in October 1943. Used as a personal transport by Maj Gen Clare Chennault, commanding general of the Fourteenth Air Force, the aircraft introduced the 'three coolies' unit insignia that was adopted by all transports and the 322nd TCS (*National Archives*)

A C-47 comes in over a DZ in northern Burma in a dive. Note the parachutes opening from the cargo dropped on this pass. Diving passes increased the aircraft's speed and reduced its vulnerability to groundfire (*National Archives*)

Future offensives launched from China and India would rely on air re-supply, as had proven so effective in New Guinea. Brigadier Orde Wingate's Chindits, who parachuted in behind enemy lines in Burma on 12 February 1943, relied exclusively on RAF transports, which flew 178 sorties and dropped 303 tons to the multi-battalion raiding force.

Following the success of this raid, Wingate realised that transport aircraft in radio contact with troops on the ground had revolutionised jungle warfare. He advocated a total restructuring of the Allied offensive so that instead of an overland advance, it would seize airheads and leapfrog forward by air to Hanoi, in Indochina.

Although this idea meshed with Gen 'Hap' Arnold's advocacy of strategic airborne invasions, there were not enough aircraft or resources, especially considering the 'Hump' commitment, in the low-priority CBI to make this strategy feasible. Therefore, Arnold promised at the Quebec conference of August 1943 that in compensation for a shortage of C-47s in-theatre, USAAF transports would aid both Wingate's next raid and an offensive in northern Burma in 1944 by Chinese forces led by US Gen Joseph Stilwell.

Two new Tenth Air Force C-47 squadrons – 1st and 2nd TCSs – arrived in India and started to fly troop re-supply missions over Burma on 3 March 1943. Reinforced by ATC, these squadrons committed four C-47s a day away from the 'Hump'.

The supply handling infrastructure in remote Assam had to be improvised, which duly slowed down operations. The 'pushers and kickers' that packed and dropped the cargo were all volunteer ground personnel who were already working flat out to keep their weary C-47s airworthy.

In June 1943, 2nd TCS, with ten C-47s, took over these missions from ATC. The 1st TCS, which commenced operations from Dinjan the following month, was reinforced by ex-ATC aircrew and assigned airdrop missions for northern Burma. The 2nd TCS, based at Sookerating, was committed to Burma airdrops in October 1943.

Japanese fighters remained a threat in Burma, and with escorts rare, some C-47 crews fitted their aircraft with improvised waist machine gun mounts.

Between these two squadrons and ATC, forces on the ground learned they could rely on USAAF air drops. With air-ground cooperation techniques improving rapidly, the C-47s' efforts shifted to northern Burma. In October, with the ending of the monsoon season, Gen Stilwell's forces – Chinese divisions, plus one US Army composite regiment known as 'Merrill's Maraud-

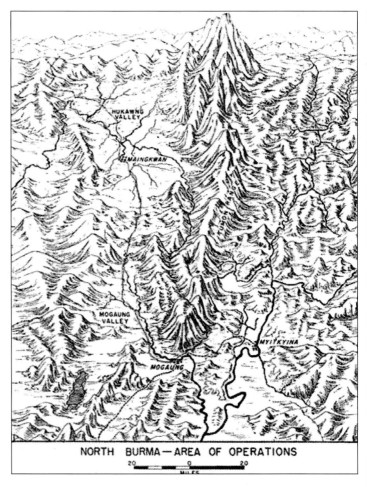

NORTH BURMA – AREA OF OPERATIONS

ers' – commenced an offensive to retake Myitkyina airfield in an effort to re-open air routes to China that could be flown at lower altitude. Seizure of the airfield would also enable work to start on the Ledo Road, connecting China with India. The success of Stilwell's offensive relied exclusively on air re-supply – 638 tons in October, increasing to 1700

North Burma Area of Operations (*US Army*)

Loading pipe into a C-47 of the 10th CCS for the Ledo Road from India to Burma (*National Archives*)

tons in December, plus a dedicated 'stovepipe' re-supply of 15 tons a day to 'Merrill's Marauders'.

This effort tied up most available C-47s in-theatre, which greatly concerned the British, who were planning offensives further south.

Tenth Air Force and RAF transport units were formed into a joint Troop Carrier Command (TCC) under USAAF Brig Gen William D Old at this time. This was in turn subordinate to the joint Eastern Air Command (EAC) under USAAF Maj Gen George E Stratemeyer. He told Washington, 'the only way we

C-47 42-32836 *Smilin' Jack* of
the 803rd Medical Air Evacuation
Squadron was a rarity, being
a dedicated medical evacuation
aircraft. With few exceptions,
USAAF Medical Air Evacuation
Squadrons provided the 'back end'
crews for troop carrier and transport
squadrons. Originally an ATC
aircraft that arrived in the CBI in
1943 and was based in Assam, this
machine was rebuilt after damage
and adorned with Red Cross
markings that only a handful of
US military aircraft carried in
combat areas on a permanent basis.
Markings included the Red Cross on
a white square above and below the
wings where there was no national
insignia, and the 'last three' digits
of the serial on the fin above the
serial itself as an aircraft number.
42-32836 was withdrawn from
use in 1945 (*National Archives*)

can supply any force that advances into Burma is by air. We must have troop carrier squadrons'. By December 1943 there were four C-47 units in the Tenth Air Force, controlled by the 433rd TCG.

USAAF C-47s were also vital to special operations in the CBI. In China, the first transports based on the far side of the 'Hump' could insert and re-supply personnel in areas where the Japanese did not have effective control. They could also retrieve downed aircrew and deliver US Office of Strategic Services (OSS), military (including weather teams) and other personnel. OSS detachments started operations among the Karens of north Burma in early 1944, and OSS officer 1Lt Joseph E Lazarsky flew on one of the early missions generated to support them;

'On 31 March 1944, I was observer aboard a C-47 from the 2nd TCS crewed by 1Lt R M Brigman (pilot), 2Lt D J Hill (co-pilot), 1Lt Hoyt E Hager, Jr (navigator) and Cpl J Meek (radio operator). The cargo was vital supplies and equipment for our party at Warang, in Burma. The ship took off from Dinjan, Assam, at 1635 hrs. Extremely unfavourable weather was encountered in the Hukawng Valley, and it was necessary to fly close to a broad thunderhead so as to cross the valley.

'After 30 minutes of flying the heavily loaded C-47 through extreme turbulence, the valley had been crossed. The weather conditions ahead appeared to be similar to those just experienced. Heavy, dark clouds hung over a ridge which was to be crossed. In my judgment, the situation justified turning back, but when I told 1Lt Brigman that the equipment was badly needed that day, he stated that he would take a chance.

'By a circuitous route across a 6000-ft ridge and through turbulent air, 1Lt Brigman flew to our destination in a valley partially covered by broken clouds. He let down over dropping ground in bad air turbulence, then under these unfavourable conditions delivered the cargo. The return trip, though with an empty ship, was arduous because of the night instrument conditions. Several days later our man in Warang reported the needed supplies and equipment were received in good condition.'

At the Cairo Conference in November 1943, China was promised a 10,000-ton monthly airlift – more than 12,000 tons arrived the following month. Plans to base B-29s in China to strike Japan further increased the ATC's 'Hump' airlift requirements. To achieve this, in addition to new aircraft – C-47s, C-46s (experiencing serviceability problems), C-87/109s (converted B-24s) and C-54s – ATC continued to build up local infrastructure. Rescue C-47s were forward based, with these being able to land or airdrop survival specialists to keep downed crews alive.

As the 1943 monsoons came to an end, the Japanese made repeated efforts to disrupt the airlift with fighter attacks and the bombing of airfields in India. While few transports were lost, these attacks forced flights onto the longer routes so as to avoid northern Burma.

In January 1944, the British troops moving along Burma's Arakan coast were forced to rely exclusively on air re-supply when the Japanese

Gen Henry 'Hap' Arnold, USAAF chief-of-staff, awards a medal to Col Philip Cochran. A veteran of North Africa, Cochran was hand-picked by Arnold to organise and lead the 1st Air Command Group in India, which provided dedicated air support for Orde Wingate's Chindits. Cochran was widely known as the model for 'Flip Corkin', a character in the then-popular comic strip *Terry and the Pirates*. Cochran used his link to Arnold to allow Wingate to receive support from other USAAF units as well as the Air Commandos (*National Archives*)

A C-47 of the 1st ACG demonstrates a unit specialty known as the 'glider snatch' at Hailakandy, in India. This tactic was used to extract both casualties and units in the Chindit campaign, along with the few surviving gliders from *Broadway*, *Chowringhee*, *Clydeside* and other forward airstrips (*National Archives*)

Army's 55th Division counterattacked the 7th Indian Division's rear echelon and divisional HQ. Although the troops were cut off, they adopted defensive positions in an area dubbed 'The Admin Box' and withstood Japanese attacks thanks to continual re-supply efforts by USAAF C-47s. Airdrops commenced on 8 February, three days after the troops had been cut off. Japanese fighters downed one transport and damaged another, thus preventing more than half the supplies from reaching the troops. Until EAC gained air superiority on 15 February, re-supply missions had to be flown at night, or with fighter escorts.

The transports eventually flew 900 sorties and delivered 1100 tons of supplies. Aside from the C-47s, 25 ATC C-46s were pulled off the 'Hump' to help with the airlift (it had taken seven days for the US Joint Chiefs of Staff in Washington, DC to approved their use!), although they lacked the C-47's reliability and proved vulnerable to ground fire. Air re-supply made 'The Admin Box' a fortress, allowing Japanese frontal attacks to be blunted by superior firepower. The enemy also threw their remaining fighters at the airlift, but they were defeated by RAF Spitfires.

However, the battle had disrupted preparations for Wingate's second offensive, including what he saw as his own private air force, the USAAF's 1st Air Commando Group (ACG). This composite unit – formed on the direct orders of Gen Arnold, and independent from EAC and withheld from TCC taskings – included a squadron of 16 C-47s and gliders. Its combat-experienced commanders, Col Philip Cochran and Lt Col John Alison, had been hand-picked by Arnold.

With the RAF unable to both support Wingate and the main force operations to the south, TCC C-47 units had to be pulled away from re-supply missions to train in glider-towing and night formation flying. Eventually, seven transport squadrons were committed to the Chindits.

Wingate had planned to use C-47s to open his offensive with an 80-glider lift into landing zones (LZs) *Broadway* and *Piccadilly*, that would then be made into airstrips. However, a shortage of C-47s meant that the gliders (overloaded Waco CG-4As, carrying 4500 lbs each rather than the standard 3750 lbs) would have to be double-towed. USAAF units had practised this in training, but it was seldom done operationally because long runways were required and C-47s had to cruise at full power. In the CBI, the use of locally procured substitute ropes increased the risk of tow lines parting, leaving gliders to crash-land in the Burmese jungle.

On 5 March the fly-in commenced, and when last-minute aerial reconnaissance revealed obstructions on *Piccadilly*, 30 minutes before take-off the entire force was diverted to *Broadway*. Of the 67 gliders towed off the ground by C-47s in the first wave, only 32 made it to a night landing at *Broadway*. Many aborted, while others suffered tow line splits.

It took 80 minutes for C-47s to climb at full throttle to the cruising altitude of 8000 ft. Approaching *Broadway*, Lt Col Alison released his glider from the lead C-47.

'Alison overboard. We'll have the bar open for you by tomorrow night', he radioed Wingate, and he proved as good as his word.

The glider force suffered heavy casualties in the night landings, but 540 troops, and their equipment, arrived, including airborne bulldozers and engineers that turned *Broadway* into a 5000-ft airstrip. The first C-47s flew in the following night with reinforcements, and on the first day of operations, 62 C-47s landed and took off from *Broadway*.

On the night of 6 March, 12 C-47s single-towed gliders to a new field, codenamed *Chowringhee*, but much of the construction equipment was lost in the landings, delaying its opening to C-47s by two days. Maj Lewis Burwell, CO of the 27th TCS, led his unit during the fly-in;

'Traffic at these strips was unbelievable. The dust was terrific. The only control was a red and green "biscuit gun". On one trip, we carried 40 fully-equipped Gurkhas, and on another, seven badly disoriented mules, with attendants. Incidentally, until you've had a scared mule frisking around in the back of your aeroplane at night, over enemy territory, you've missed one of life's rare sensations.

'Our loads grossed as much as 4000 lbs over airline maximums. The temporary strips were considerably shorter than runways in the States, and were as rough as a Minsky matinee. Landing lights were out of the question. The only possible technique was to line her up, hold the airspeed steady, aim for the first flare pots, then pray and sweat. The glow from the exhaust stacks of the ship in front told you if your interval was too close. Nothing told you if the guy behind was too close.

'For concealment and security against air and ground attack, the strips had been selected to permit only one approach – like giant caves with the roofs knocked out. Regardless of wind, take-off was made in the direction opposite to landing. The high peaks that rimmed one end and both sides made "over shooting" simply out of the question. There were no pull up and go around procedures, no second choice. Yet in spite of these apparently impossible conditions, the safety record was phenomenal. The only casualties were in the initial blacked-out glider landings, and the only aircraft damaged were in a dust cloud tangle at *Chowringhee*.'

The decision was soon made to fly the main Chindit striking force into *Broadway*, and in a six-day operation, 9000 troops, 1300 pack animals, 250 tons of supplies and a battery each of Bofors 40 mm and pack howitzers arrived. Losses were low, but included Wingate, killed in a B-25 crash. Maj Burwell saw him just before his last take-off;

'The days were getting hot. Sleeping was difficult. Each night the weather across the mountains was a little thicker. There were more thunderstorms to dodge. One night the turbulence was especially severe. Co-pilot Brooks and I squirmed and wiggled our way into *Broadway*, on instruments practically the entire distance. Gen Wingate was there preparing to return to India in

Maj Lewis Burwell, CO of the 27th TCS, waves from the pilot's seat of his C-47, *Eadie II*. The 27th became the first transport squadron to be permanently based in China after it had supported the Chindits and participated in the airlifts to Imphal and Myitkyina, in Burma. The undercockpit Rebecca antenna is of the early design, recognisable by light-coloured vertical elements. Burwell was a strong and forceful commanding officer of a unit that, alongside the 315th TCS, joined the Air Commandos and the RAF in supporting the Chindits while the 1st and 2nd TCS worked with Stillwell's forces to the north in 1944. In 1945 the 27th moved to China to make possible the successful Chinese counter-offensive along the Salween River (*National Archives*)

Chindits – soldiers of the King's Liverpool Regiment (Pvte William McEwen in left foreground), West African Frontier Force and Indian Army personnel – wait for a night fly-in at Langalat forward base, in India. Four 27th TCS C-47s are on the flightline (*National Archives*)

A 2nd ACG Waco CG-4A glider is seen en route to northern Burma behind a C-47 (out of shot) in single tow configuration in February 1945. The initial Chindit insertions, using double tows and flown at night, were much more challenging. The US-built CG-4As were vital to Chindit operations because there was no British glider capability in the CBI. The Horsa glider was not only too big for Burmese LZs, it was unsuitable for the moist tropical climate, as its plywood construction tended to come unglued (*National Archives*)

one of Cochran's B-25s. He asked about the weather. We told him we weren't going to return until after midnight when the thunderstorms had begun to dissipate. Three days later the burned wreckage of his ship was found on a mountain side near the Burma-India border. His famous sun helmet was still intact.'

C-47s continued to bring in supplies to *Broadway* and *Chowringhee* (evacuated on 10 March), as well as flying sorties for the Chindits. Another airstrip – *Aberdeen* – was opened after six gliders with engineers were towed in on the night of 22 March, while ground columns captured another airfield (*White City*).

Because many of the DZs were in close proximity to Japanese flak positions, the majority of missions were flown at night. Gliders were often used to deliver equipment – 1st ACG C-47s alone flew more than 90 glider missions in the following two months – and were later picked up from the LZs by hook-equipped C-47s.

In late March, a Chindit force was inserted in the Kawlin-Wunthe area in five gliders and, mission accomplished, was extracted the same way. Air casualty evacuation was also one of the major improvements from the first Chindit operation. Air mobility also allowed the force to be concentrated and moved faster than the enemy could respond. But other claims on transports in the CBI limited the Chindits' ability to sustain operations. Nevertheless, their withdrawal was not completed until August.

Gen Stilwell's concurrent offensive into northern Burma, slowed by lack of re-supply during the Chindit fly-ins, was reinforced by an additional Chinese division brought in by returning 'Hump' flights from China to Sookerating in late March. From there, in a seven-day airlift on 5-12 April, C-47s of the 1st TCS, with reinforcement from other units, brought 7250 Chinese troops into battle in 203 sorties, An additional 280 re-supply sorties were also flown to the forces in northern Burma.

While these operations were taking place, the Japanese launched their decisive offensive into India on 10 March. Many of the Allied transports were still operating further north, supporting Stilwell or flying night missions in support of the Chindits at the time. The Japanese succeeded in wrong-footing the Allies, who were deployed for an advance in south Burma. Rapidly advancing, enemy forces cut off a large concentration of troops in Dimapur, Imphal and Kohima. It was the 'Admin Box' on a much larger scale, and air re-supply again became vital. Japanese reserve air power from throughout Southeast Asia supported the offensive.

Maj Burwell explained that 'the siege of Imphal developed rapidly. All night, every night, we'd see long enemy convoys moving toward India on the few east-west roads in Burma. Zeros popped over the Chin Hills above the Imphal plain every morning with the sun. Every return trip from Burma had to cross this unhealthy patch of sky. The "dawn came up out of China" and we raced it home'.

With Allied fighters needed to combat Japanese air attacks, C-47s – reinforced by bombers – had to fly airlift missions without escorts. The Supreme Allied Commander South East Asia Theatre, Adm Lord Louis Mountbatten, wanted 30 ATC C-47s to be diverted from the 'Hump' within 72 hours, but Washington allocated 20 C-46s instead. The Indian 5th and 7th Divisions were quickly flown into Imphal, whilst Allied forward positions – including beleaguered Kohima – were sustained by air re-supply. 1Lt Ralph C De Dastro of the 27th TCS described the night airdrop missions his unit flew in the absence of fighter escorts;

'The missions to feed these men were to be flown at night, thus lessening the danger of interception, and making it difficult for their intelligences to find out what was going on. At our base in Sylhet, from red mud revetments, along winding narrow taxiways, our transports made their way to the runway. Their opened doors revealed rations packed neatly in packs, with the parachute folded and tied over them.

'On all three dropping missions, the ships carried an eight-man crew consisting of the pilot, co-pilot, navigator, crew chief, radio operator and three men in the back of the aeroplane whose job it was to push the packs out on a signal from the pilot. As one can readily imagine, the ships were very heavily loaded. As the pilots muttered "Mixtures rich, tail wheel locked, cowl flaps trail", the "old faithfuls" rolled down their grey cement path, gathering speed and more speed until they were airborne into the night. They climbed slowly, but unfalteringly, to their assigned altitudes, headed east towards Imphal, crossed the swamps, flew on into the darkness of the night that could be felt. The blackness was incredible – nothing could be seen in either the sky or on the ground.

'The first visible landmark was the great winding Chindwin River. The aeroplanes flew on, the minutes dragged by, the navigators, poring over their tables, stared at their maps, checked and rechecked their courses, figured their ETAs (estimated time of arrival) to within seconds and hurriedly went forward to their equally worried pilots. Suddenly, like a light from heaven, a signal was seen below. The code letter for the night was flashed and a proper answer received. The ships let down slowly, with great caution, as so much of that territory was unsurveyed, and there was no definite knowledge as to the altitude of the surrounding terrain.

'Above the gigantic trees of that dense jungle, the aeroplanes flew their drop patterns. As they reached the small clearing between the trees, the bell rang in the back of the aeroplane and the three men pushed out the packs of eagerly awaited rations.'

By late March, the Japanese offensive had ground to a halt, but Allied ground supply routes remained cut. Stilwell's drive on Myitkyina required transport support if it was to succeed before the monsoons arrived, so Mountbatten again asked for more ATC transports. This time, Washington turned him down. However, the Combined Chiefs of Staff committee ordered four USAAF C-47 squadrons (the 64th TCG) plus an RAF Dakota unit from Italy to India in an emergency deployment that was to last until May, but turned out to be required until late June.

For the aircrew of the 64th TCG, transferred from Italy, the monsoon and the presence of enemy fighters were both unfamiliar. On 1 May, a formation of eight 64th TCG C-47s was attacked by Japanese fighters. Seven survived and carried out their missions. The eighth C-47

(42-24376 of the 35th TCS) was being flown by 1Lt Ellis W Widney, along with 2Lt Peter A Machnik (co-pilot), TSgt Don C Hays (crew chief) and Sgt John Knag (radio operator). They also had a British passenger on board. Widney reported;

'At 0840 hrs, about 25 miles south and west of Palel at an altitude of 1000 ft, three "Oscar Is" attacked my aeroplane, firing from the right side of the C-47. The first bursts set the load of empty gasoline drums on fire and scored hits on the tail surfaces, severing some of the control cables. I drove the ship to the deck and attempted to land it, cutting both engines. The ship bounced off a small knoll into a swamp, tearing away the undercarriage, and then bellied into the swamp at a speed of 150 miles an hour. The crew, including one British passenger, and I escaped through the forward escape hatch of the blazing ship.

'As the last man crawled to safety from the blazing inferno that the airplane now was, the three "Oscars" returned, strafing. Each "Oscar" made a pass at the aeroplane and departed. We proceeded through the swamp, with mud and water up to our waists.'

Everyone made it back to Allied lines, and a second C-47 survived a mid-air collision with an attacking Japanese fighter.

Additional reinforcements, including the 1st Combat Cargo Group (CCG), were despatched from US bases via the South Atlantic route. The combat cargo units had the same capabilities as troop carriers, but had 25-aircraft squadrons (troop carrier squadrons had 16, increased from 13, with few units having the opportunity to become over-strength in aircraft as many did in the ETO). They also had less organic support capability, depending instead on the group's four airfield units (where troop carrier squadrons each had their own ground echelon).

A further 100 C-47s were flown out from the US individually and formed into the 3rd CCG on arrival in India. They lacked pre-deployment unit training, but once thrown into combat alongside more experienced crews, they were soon making up a vital part of the airlift effort. Indeed, they took over from the 64th TCG, which returned to Italy to prepare for the invasion of southern France in June.

Despite the withdrawal of ATC C-46s (ten in late April and the remainder in early June), the pre-monsoon airlift proved a success. In addition to continuing the re-supply of the Chindits and Stilwell, 58,000 Allied troops were re-supplied by air while 12,000 reinforcements and 32,000 tons of supplies were flown in. In addition to 30,000 non-essential personnel, 15,000 sick and wounded had been evacuated by the time the Imphal siege ended in June.

In northern Burma, airdrops to the forces closing in on Myitkyina remained highly dangerous, as reported by pilot 1Lt Robert M Brigman of the 2nd TCS;

'On Thursday, 20 April 1944, I took off from Dinjan Field, India, in C-47 41-19497 at 0910 hrs, on a Galahad mission (dedicated re-supply to Merrill's' Marauders). We arrived over

Everyone walked away from this C-47 which overran a runway at Shadazup, in Burma, in August 1944. The aircraft was subsequently salvaged (*National Archives*)

The end result of a taxiing accident at Myitkyina during the May 1944 fly-in. Such accidents were commonplace during the frenetic operations which followed the seizing of this vital airstrip in Burma. However, the construction of a tower, a navigation beacon and an air traffic control facility – all flown in by C-47s – soon enabled the airfield to safely sustain a tremendous amount of traffic, despite the presence of the Japanese nearby until August 1944 (*National Archives*)

This 1st ACG C-47 was photographed on 5 December 1944 whilst taking part in Operation *Grubworm* – one of the airlifts of Chinese forces to China after securing objectives in northern Burma. The Chinese reliance on muscle power as opposed to the 'high technology' represented by the C-47s was much commented on by the Allies at the time (*National Archives*)

the target at 1030 hrs and proceeded to drop our supplies. The air was rough, and we were also getting a strong blast of prop wash from a C-47 in front of us.

'On the next to last approach to the target, we were letting down for our drop when we hit very bad prop wash which threw us into a very steep turn towards the left. In trying to correct for this, some or all of the parapacks were thrown out by the motion of the aeroplane, and at least one lodged itself on our tail section. The left stabiliser and elevator were jammed, causing the tail of the aeroplane to toss violently up and down, forcing the C-47 into a gradually steepening turn towards the left which I was at first unable to control.

'After telling the co-pilot, 2Lt Ralph L Harmon, to have the crew bail out, I realised that we were too low for jumping and tried to get them to brace themselves for a crash. However, no one could hear me, and since the motion of the aeroplane was so violent that the crew could not put their 'chutes on, 2Lt Harmon succeeded in grabbing two men and pulling them down to the floor of the cargo compartment with him.

'While all this was going on, I tried to recover from the turn. Succeeding in part, I put on full power, causing the nose of the ship to drop. I brought it back to cruising power and headed as best I could for the strip at the target. We kept losing altitude steadily, and our air speed kept falling off from 105 mph with full power to approximately 60 mph before we crashed. While we were about ten feet from the ground, the snared 'chute let go and I pulled the wheel back into my lap to stall the aeroplane in. I relaxed as much as possible in preparation for the crash. We hit the ground, bounced once and slid for about 20 ft, then stopped. The ship hit the ground at approximately 1045 hrs.'

The entire crew walked away from the crash-landing – a demonstration of the ruggedness of the C-47 and the hazards of the resupply mission, even in the absence of enemy action – with Brigman sustaining minor injuries.

On 17 May, days before the monsoon would curtail air operations, Merrill's Marauders seized Myitkyina airfield. Their first action was to call for C-47s, with an initial four-ship airdrop including a forward control team and marker panels for a follow-on nine-glider lift. By the night of the 17th, the airfield was open to C-47s. The result was a concentrated fly-in to secure the site as a base for further operations. By 19 May, C-47s – including ATC reinforcements – had flown in 4000

troops, 500 tons of supplies, and an anti-aircraft battery. While the enemy would hold out nearby until August, the airfield was quickly expanded and turned into a major way-point for supply flights to China.

Despite the divided command structure and unsure strategic dimension of the CBI, effective inter-allied cooperation emerged. The EAC's TCC, pulled in multiple directions, disbanded at the end of May. Its US assets went to the joint Third Tactical Air Force, the Tenth Air Force, or, later, to the inter-allied Combat Cargo Task Force (CCTF). Despite the continued issues with ATC reinforcement, CCTF was an effective central command for airlift over southern Burma, with the USAAF handling missions in northern Burma and China. The Tenth Air Force activated its own Air Cargo Headquarters.

When the monsoons ended in October, Allied forces launched an offensive aimed at driving the Japanese first from their spring gains and then out of Burma. This was made possible by air-ground cooperation.

In addition to keeping China in the war, the 'Hump' route had to supply the expanded Fourteenth Air Force, now on the offensive against the Japanese. The Twentieth Air Force's B-29s arrived in China in mid-1944, and initially had to be pressed into service as transports, making several flights to India to bring back bombs and fuel for every mission launched. Burma operations and B-29 requirements (2000 tons) had reduced the cargo available for China to 7500 tons a month. Despite the monsoon, in May-October 14,000 transport landings delivered 40,000+ tons of supplies. Expanding the ground facilities in the monsoon rains was a tremendous feat, and at times transports were stacked up for hours over airfields waiting for stuck aircraft to be cleared from runways.

Brig (later Maj) Gen William Tunner took over ATC's airlift in September 1944. His arrival coincided with a major build-up of the command – from 369 transports in August 1944, it more than doubled in size in the next year – and the opening of more direct air routes over north Burma. He built on this by establishing a system of airline-style Production Line Maintenance at Indian bases (rather than each transport having its own groundcrew), imposing stringent flight safety standards and improving navigation aids. He succeeded in halving the attrition rate.

A C-47 of the 1st CCG carries out an airdrop to a DZ in Burma defended by a British Bofors gun on 6 December 1944 (*National Archives*)

Brig Gen William Tunner took command of 'Hump' operations after its 1943-44 crises and, in its final year, turned it into one of the great strategic air power successes of World War 2. Tunner later used this experience to successfully command the Berlin Airlift, turning that into one of the great strategic air power successes of the Cold War (*National Archives*)

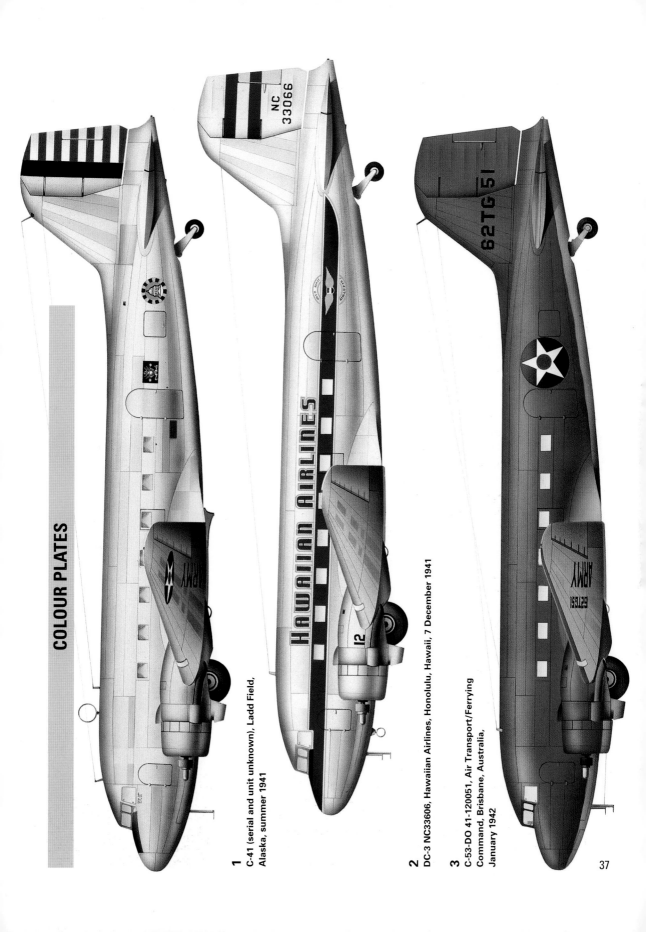

COLOUR PLATES

1
C-41 (serial and unit unknown), Ladd Field,
Alaska, summer 1941

2
DC-3 NC33606, Hawaiian Airlines, Honolulu, Hawaii, 7 December 1941

3
C-53-DO 41-120051, Air Transport/Ferrying
Command, Brisbane, Australia,
January 1942

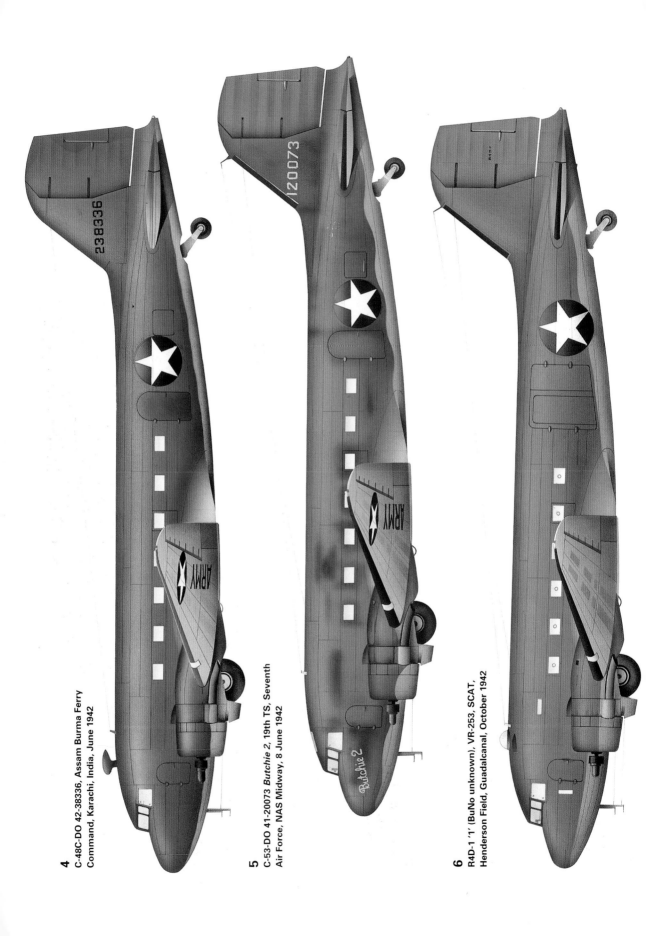

4
C-48C-DO 42-38336, Assam Burma Ferry
Command, Karachi, India, June 1942

5
C-53-DO 41-20073 *Butchie 2*, 19th TS, Seventh
Air Force, NAS Midway, 8 June 1942

6
R4D-1 '1' (BuNo unknown), VR-253, SCAT,
Henderson Field, Guadalcanal, October 1942

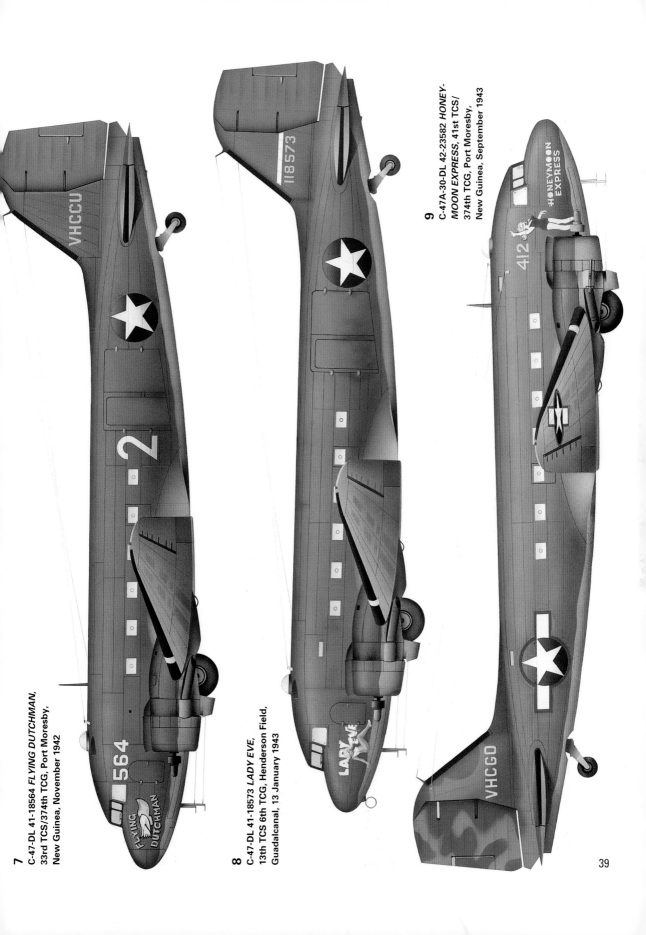

7
C-47-DL 41-18564 *FLYING DUTCHMAN*,
33rd TCS/374th TCG, Port Moresby,
New Guinea, November 1942

8
C-47-DL 41-18573 *LADY EVE*,
13th TCS 6th TCG, Henderson Field,
Guadalcanal, 13 January 1943

9
C-47A-30-DL 42-23582 *HONEY-MOON EXPRESS*, 41st TCS/
374th TCG, Port Moresby,
New Guinea, September 1943

39

10
R4D-1 '5-R-105' (BuNo unknown),
VR-5, NATS, Adak, late 1943

11
C-47A-35-DL 42-23880 *SURE SKIN*,
68th TCS/433rd TCG, Port Moresby,
New Guinea, December 1943

12
R4D-5 BuNo 17136 (USAAF 42-92842), VMR-352,
John Rogers Field, Hawaii, August 1944

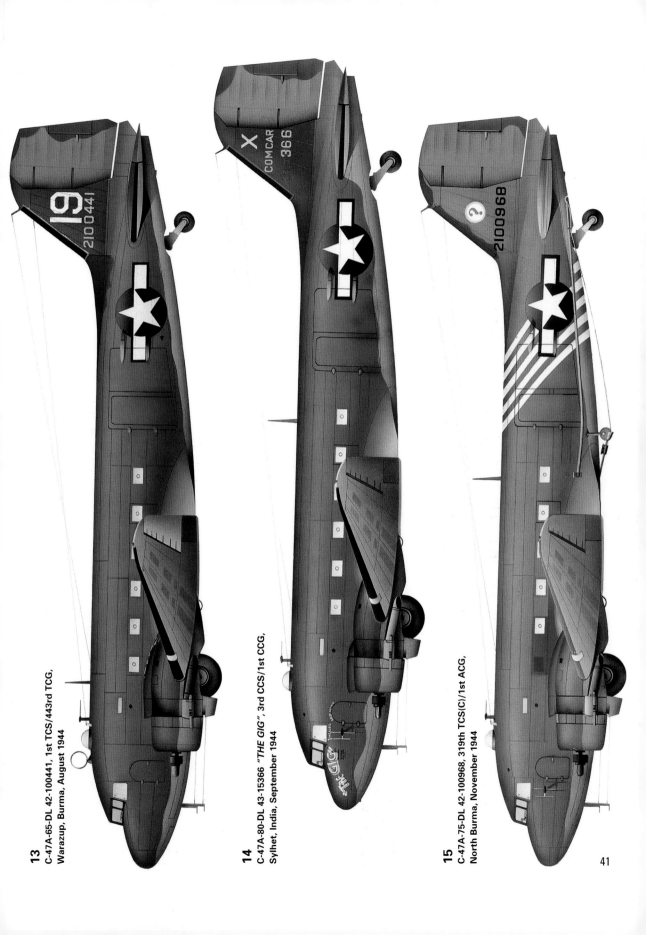

13
C-47A-65-DL 42-100441, 1st TCS/443rd TCG,
Warazup, Burma, August 1944

14
C-47A-80-DL 43-15366 "THE GIG", 3rd CCS/1st CCG,
Sylhet, India, September 1944

15
C-47A-75-DL 42-100968, 319th TCS(CI)/1st ACG,
North Burma, November 1944

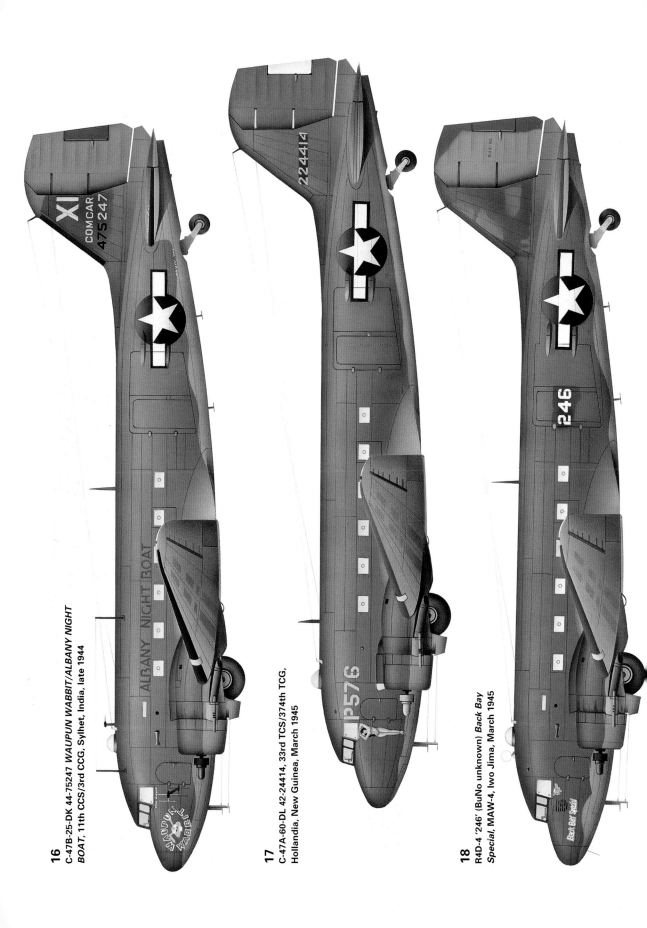

16
C-47B-25-DK 44-75247 *WAUPUN WABBIT/ALBANY NIGHT BOAT*, 11th CCS/3rd CCG, Sylhet, India, late 1944

17
C-47A-60-DL 42-24414, 33rd TCS/374th TCG, Hollandia, New Guinea, March 1945

18
R4D-4 '246' (BuNo unknown) *Back Bay Special*, MAW-4, Iwo Jima, March 1945

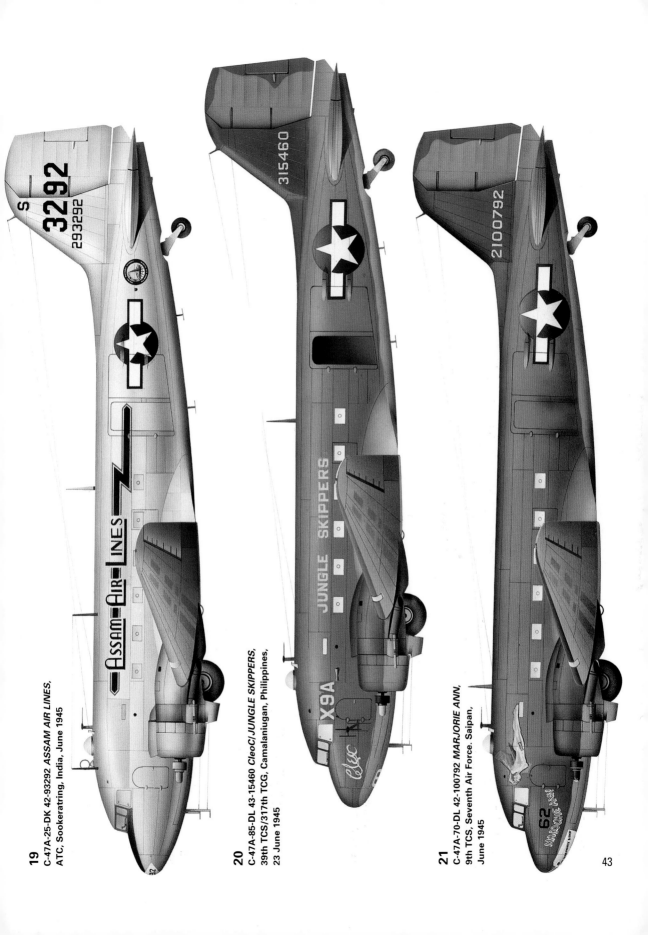

19
C-47A-25-DK 42-93292 *ASSAM AIR LINES*,
ATC, Sookeratring, India, June 1945

20
C-47A-85-DL 43-15460 *CleoCl JUNGLE SKIPPERS*,
39th TCS/317th TCG, Camalaniugan, Philippines,
23 June 1945

21
C-47A-70-DL 42-100792 *MARJORIE ANN*,
9th TCS, Seventh Air Force. Saipan,
June 1945

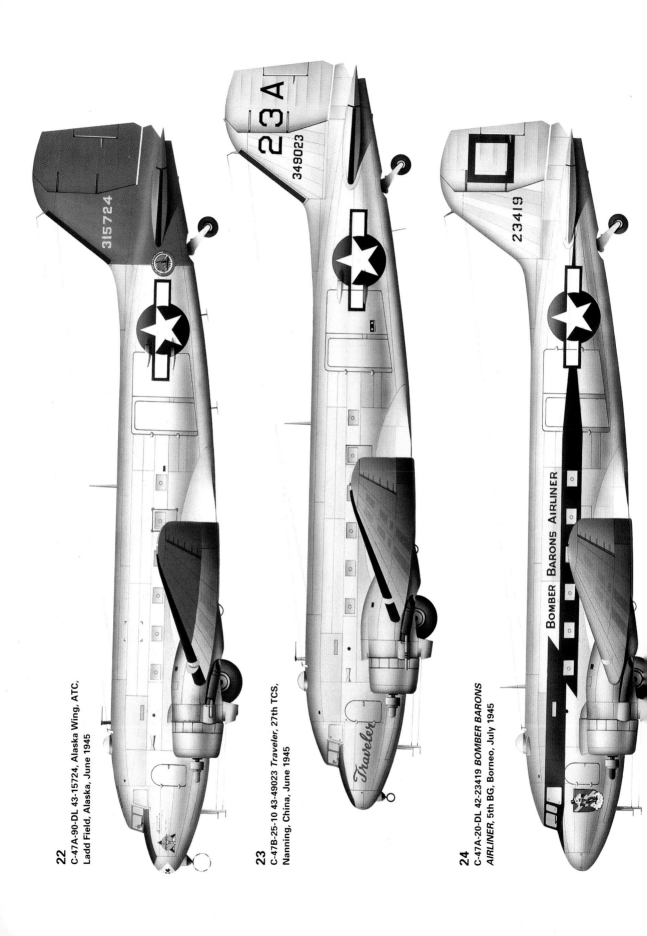

22
C-47A-90-DL 43-15724, Alaska Wing, ATC,
Ladd Field, Alaska, June 1945

23
C-47B-25-10 43-49023 *Traveler*, 27th TCS,
Nanning, China, June 1945

24
C-47A-20-DL 42-23419 *BOMBER BARONS
AIRLINER*, 5th BG, Borneo, July 1945

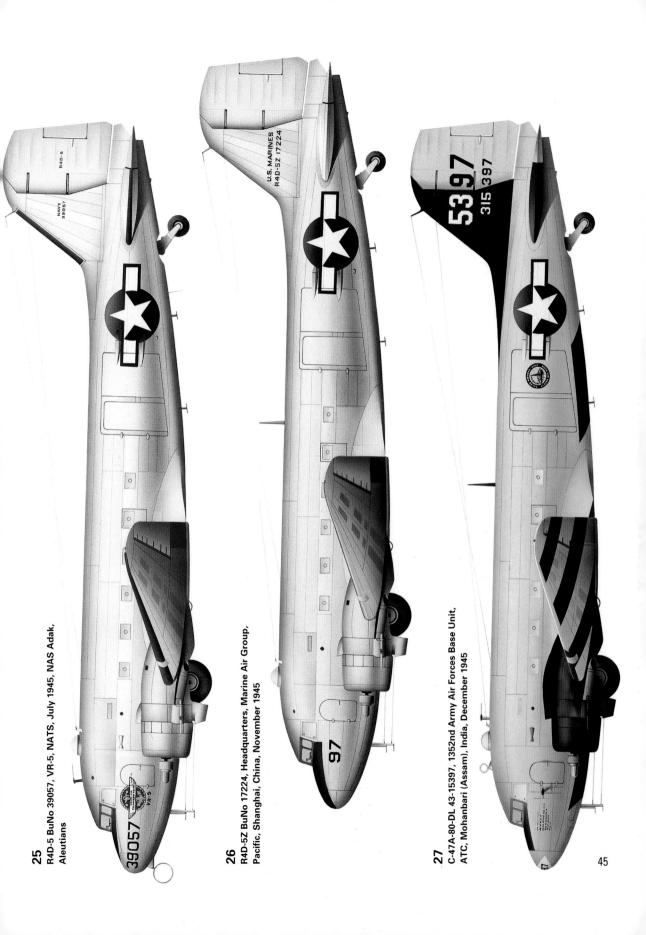

25
R4D-5 BuNo 39057, VR-5, NATS, July 1945, NAS Adak,
Aleutians

26
R4D-5Z BuNo 17224, Headquarters, Marine Air Group,
Pacific, Shanghai, China, November 1945

27
C-47A-80-DL 43-15397, 1352nd Army Air Forces Base Unit,
ATC, Mohanbari (Assam), India, December 1945

28
C-47B-30-DK 44-76458, 332nd TCS, Shanghai,
China, December 1945

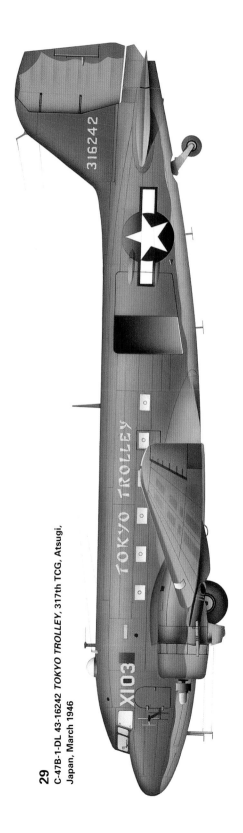

29
C-47B-1-DL 43-16242 *TOKYO TROLLEY*, 317th TCG, Atsugi,
Japan, March 1946

30

30
C-47C-10-DK 42-108868 *The Duck*, 54th TCS, Eleventh Air
Force, Ladd Field, Alaska, 15 April 1945

30

28

22

PACIFIC THEATRES 1942-44

There was no single 'Pacific Theatre' as such. Aside from the SWPA – firmly under control of Gen MacArthur – the remainder was divided into 'areas' under the control of Adm Chester Nimitz's Pacific Ocean Areas headquarters in Hawaii. Each had different operational challenges for the C-47/R4Ds that operated in them.

In the North Pacific, the Eleventh Air Force's C-47-equipped 42nd and 54th TCSs operated throughout the Aleutians campaign in 1942-43, backed up by ATC, which extended its routes down the Aleutian chain as far as Adak and Shemya. NATS was also active in-theatre, equipped with chartered airliners that allowed it to sustain air operations in some of the worst weather in the world with limited infrastructure and support. Aleutian operations were as demanding as any in the war against Japan.

As long as the Japanese had fighters in the Aleutians, transport missions to the outer islands were flown with P-40 escorts on those occasions that there was less than five-tenths cloud cover (used for quick evasive action). No transports were lost to fighters, but the weather and terrain often proved lethal.

Airdrops – first by bombers and then by C-47s – were made to ground troops in the fighting on Attu. A parachute assault by the US-Canadian 1st Special Service Force, to be dropped by C-47s staging through Adak, was the planned as part of Operation *Cottage* (the invasion of Kiska) in August 1943. Both units deployed most of their aircraft to Amchitka to train for the invasion, but it was cancelled when it appeared that the Japanese had evacuated Kiska. After the Japanese withdrawal, the 54th TCS remained in-theatre.

Navigation aids and additional training eventually made operations possible in conditions that would have grounded all aircraft in 1942.

Bottom
The Pacific Areas map produced by the US Army shows the vastness of this theatre (*US Army*)

Below
A US Navy NATS R4D-1 of VR-4 flies over spectacular terrain – 'rock-stuffed-clouds' – on Kodiak Island in 1943 during the height of the Aleutians campaign. Note that the national insignia is carried in six positions (*National Archives*)

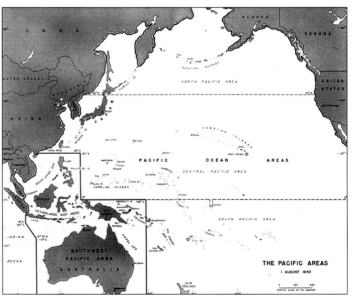

THE PACIFIC AREAS
I AUGUST 1942

1Lt Lawrence P Solomon of the 54th TCS described a 'routine' mission from Attu to Elmendorf field, in Alaska;

'As I got my stuff together and shoved it into a worn and dilapidated musette bag, I thought about the trip I would fly the following morning. Six months ago, I would have been on pins and needles, as the saying goes, to go out. Now, for some unknown reason, it was just another routine trip down the "Chain" to Attu, and once there it would be a routine trip up the "Chain" to Elmendorf. How would the weather be? Would we have an eventful trip? These questions popped off of my mind like peas off of armour plate. The weather was a question that wasn't answered until after take-off. The eventfulness of the trip I could have bet on, and given odds that it would be the same as always – out and back, unless something happened, which it never did.

'The things that had so startled me when I first came to the theatre were now routine. Landings and take-offs in the foulest weather, let-downs onto island fields that would have bewildered a Grasshopper pilot – these things were mere routine now, and nothing more. Adak was my backyard and taxiing at Attu was simply worming my car through the maze of the "Loop" back home.

'There is nothing much at 10,000 ft over Kenai, nothing but clouds, darkness and a noticeable lack of air-ground radio communication. The routine impressions were gone now, lost in the work of ascertaining position, check and cross-check, and flying the aeroplane, lost in the knowledge of 11,000 ft of solid rock a few miles to the right.

'A broad "N" from the Iliamna (radio) range immediately changed to an "A" and then to an "on course" – winding up, it emitted all three signals at once! This verified our position as being right in the middle of Bruin Bay Pass, and on course. Had we been anywhere else, we'd have gotten a reasonable signal. To the right were some very rugged mountains, and to the left, Seattle, San Francisco and Los Angeles. Bruin Bay Pass, where the wind blows from all points of the compass at once and puts the "willi" in williwaw (a violent wind, staple of Aleutians weather).

'The weather office is the pilots' Mecca, and any one weather office on the "Chain" is the prototype of all the others. Here, there is much

Mail is transferred from an R4D-5 of NATS' VR-5 to a dogsled for final delivery at NAS Kodiak, Alaska, in 1944. Note that the inside of the cargo doors have been repainted a darker (green?) shade than their usual zinc chromate green. The inside of the forward cargo door also has a survival kit affixed to it. This type of mounting was common throughout the Pacific, and was often accompanied by an extra life-raft on the inside of the larger cargo door. Finally, the aircraft's BuNo, 30147, has been applied much larger (and lower on the fin) than was usual on R4Ds (*National Archives*)

On Attu, in the Aleutians, as with most other liberated Pacific islands, the 'first aeroplane in' was a C-47 or, in this case, an R4D of NATS. Standing behind its wing on Attu are (from left to right), its pilot, Cdr Storrs, co-pilot (unidentified) Lt H L Dalgren (operations) and Lt A D Lindley (NAS Attu executive officer) (*National Archives*)

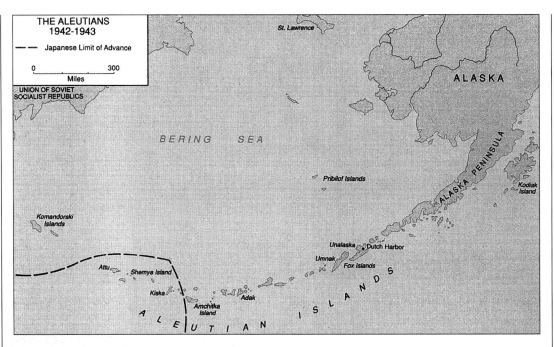

THE ALEUTIANS
1942-1943

‐‐‐‐‐ Japanese Limit of Advance

0   300
Miles

UNION OF SOVIET
SOCIALIST REPUBLICS

ALASKA

BERING SEA

Pribilof Islands

Kodiak
Island

ALASKA PENINSULA

Komandorski
Islands

Unalaska   Dutch Harbor
Umnak
Fox Islands

Attu   Shemya Island

Kiska   Adak

Amchitka
Island

A L E U T I A N   I S L A N D S

A wartime map of the Aleutians theatre in 1942-43, as produced by the US Army (*US Army*)

A C-47 of the Alaska ATC Wing's Search and Rescue Flight flies past the peaks in the Denali area of Alaska in untypically clear weather in 1944. Such ATC flights predated the organisation of Emergency Rescue Squadrons by the USAAF. Because the latter introduced the OA-10 amphibian so late in the war, C-47s airdropping rafts or supplies provided the backbone of USAAF rescue efforts for much of World War 2 (*National Archives*)

discussion and argument, plotting of fronts upon maps, tracking of pressure areas, dissemination of pilot's reports – all of this and more, terminating in the ultimate decision that Aleutian weather is unpredictable. The pilots congregate in the office and mull over the sequences, trying to find some portent of the weather ahead.

'We came into the weather office while the ship was being gassed, tossing our flight clearance onto the table. Near the back of the room, the teletype machines played their perpetual racket and the GIs were decoding the weather as it came in. Exchanging greetings with the weatherman on duty, we looked over the sequence – it wasn't good, and it wasn't bad, just an average day. There was ceiling and visibility, and the wind – not a lot of the former and more than we would have preferred of the latter. It was plenty good enough though, and we were pleased indeed, for we had expected to spend some hours there "sweating it out".

'The weatherman, true to his trade, was verbose, and we bent respectful ears to his esoteric analysis. The business of putting the weather on the clearance, taking a last minute look at the sequence, and exchanging a few well-worn jokes with the 'rainmaker' was finally finished and we went out to our ship.

'We climbed out through the overcast to altitude, but failed to get "on top". On course and droning along through the soup, we looked for icing and turbulence, and waited to cross some of the intersections –

points to call in position reports. The intersections are made by the crossing of one or more (AM radio or radio range) beam legs, and for the most part any one intersection is never entirely in the same position two days running. This can be disconcerting at times, but it does bring in the element of surprise now and then. Trying to hit an ETA between Cold Bay and Atka is like getting a dime out of an Officer's Club slot-machine. AACS (Alaska Air Control Sector) makes up its own ETA for you, however, and yours is requested, I believe, just to make you feel like a dammed fool when you miss it by five minutes.

'Arriving at our destination, we had hardly finished cutting the engines, when the Air Freight Officer was breathing heavily over my shoulder. The Air Freight Officer is an enigmatic person who is disgusted when you're eastbound and he has freight for the west, and equally put out when the situation is vice versa. I shoved our manifest at him, and requested a load for the east in accordance with my orders. He grudgingly assented to give it to me, mumbling under his breath at the same time about three loads he had waiting to shuttle. Ignoring his mutterings, we made arrangements for take-off, and then struck out for the mess hall.

'Some 12 flying hours later, and one day later, our wheels touched the runway at Elmendorf. The round trip had been completed without an incident, and two thoughts were predominant in my mind. One was to pick up a handful of mail that I hoped was awaiting me and the other was to get "home" as soon as possible and go to sleep. In a few days I would be going on another hop – best to get as much "sack" as possible before then.

'Dropping our intelligence material off, we headed for our quarters, and then, in retrospect, the trip seemed again mere routine. In a few days I would be sweating it out again, anxious about the next trip, which might be more than routine.'

Air- and groundcrew load a precious cargo – a B-24 main gear tyre – into a C-53 in Alaska in late 1942. The fighter and bomber squadrons of the Eleventh Air Force relied on airlift support to allow them to sustain operations from remote forward airstrips in the Aleutians. The ability to successfully conduct such supply flights in highly challenging weather was critical to US operations throughout this forgotten theatre in 1942-43 (*National Archives*)

CENTRAL PACIFIC

The Central Pacific offensive, opening with the invasions of the Marshalls and Gilberts in 1943, involved joint USAAF and Marine Corps transport operations. Hawaii-based Seventh Air Force C-47s and R4Ds of VMJ-252 had previously supported Marine Corps units defending Midway Island during the decisive battle there in June 1942, and operated to forward island bases. These aircraft – supplemented by bombers – had been committed on air transport missions to islands on

Aircraft '657' of the 19th TCS undergoes an engine change at a forward island base in 1943. This Hawaii-based unit was dubbed 'Southern Cross Airways', and aside from transport flights, it also supplied pathfinder aircraft for fighter and bomber squadrons flying down the ferry route to combat zones as far away as New Caledonia. 19th TCS C-47s occasionally encountered, and evaded, Japanese reconnaissance aircraft (*National Archives*)

Built as a C-53-DO, 41-20046 of ATC's Pacific Wing featured a unique two-tone camouflage scheme as seen here at Kwajalein in March 1944. Fitted with a C-47 door, this aircraft spent 20 years in civilian service with Hawaiian Airlines until eventually scrapped in the 1970s (*National Archives*)

the southern air routes to Samoa, Fiji, Australia and New Zealand. Now, with the benefit of Guadalcanal lessons, these units became part of the Transport Aircraft Group (TAG), a joint air transport organisation for the Central Pacific formed on the model of SCAT.

Carrying out priority cargo and casualty evacuation missions, TAG C-47/R4Ds operated to airstrips on Tarawa, Kwajalein and many other islands soon after the invasions there. The swift completion of airstrips by engineers was followed by a fly-in of combat aircraft, led by C-47/R4Ds and, until surface transport could provide bulk delivery, sustained by airlift of fuel and munitions. While bypassed Japanese garrisons lacked fighters to threaten transports, they still constituted en route hazards. A few transport crews literally 'moonlighted' as unofficial night bombers, detouring to roll a few 'borrowed' bombs out the cargo door over these islands.

During the advance into the Marianas in mid-1944, as elsewhere in the Pacific, there were not enough four-engined transports. C-47s flew long-range airdrop missions, usually with in-cabin tanks, to frontline troops. C-47s were also used for DDT spraying to prevent malarial outbreaks. As islands were secured, ATC and NATS extended their routes forward.

In the South Pacific Area, the advance up the Solomons chain reflected the patterns established and lessons learned in New Guinea and on Guadalcanal. C-47/R4Ds arrived early, making forward tactical air operations possible, (often serving as lead ships for ferry flights) and back-loading casualties.

Still more C-47s flew out from California to New Caledonia and Espiritu Santo, followed by the 403rd TCG Headquarters to take control of them, and the now-veteran 13th TCS under SCAT control as the

Thirteenth Air Force's only TCG (the Seventh and Eleventh Air Forces had only provisional TCGs).

SCAT supported the invasion of the Russell Islands in February 1943, flying in as soon as the first airstrip opened. The landings on New Georgia in June 1943 put additional demands on SCAT, with C-47s and R4Ds flying in priority supplies and making supply drops to troops in the frontline. Once again, the experience of the New Guinea campaign and lessons from Guadalcanal were applied throughout these operations. Munda field soon opened on New Georgia, followed by airstrips on Vella Lavella (invaded in August) and Bougainville (November), and these bases were used as forward bases to support ground operations with supply airdrops and medical evacuation. Such missions in turn made possible further advances. And with SCAT increasing in size throughout this period, its operations were duly divided into Northern, Middle and Southern Areas.

Connecting these transport operations with the US were ATC and NATS. ATC started the first inter-theatre medical evacuation flights, from India and Australia to the US, in early 1943. While four-engined transports were used for long overwater crossings whenever possible, their scarcity meant that C-47s had to fly many of these missions well into 1944. The first flights proved difficult to coordinate, especially with

SCAT Marine Corps R4D '64' (the aircraft number painted both on its nacelles and nose) is marshalled on the ground in the Solomons in 1943 (*National Archives*)

Marine Corps R4D '36' suffered a left main gear collapse at Abemama in 1944 (*National Archives*)

An R4D takes off on yet another mission from the airfield at Espiritu Santo in 1944. This base had played a key role as the intermediate field for the 1942 re-supply effort to Guadalcanal (*National Archives*)

A C-47 or R4D transport rests between flights in the Marshall Islands in 1944 – perhaps the aircraft's crew are being driven out to it in that Jeep? As US forces advanced into the Marshalls, a Hawaii-headquartered joint transport organisation was established in order to build on the success of SCAT in the Solomons (*OWI photo from Author's Collection*)

on-the-ground patient care. ATC had to build a medical infrastructure to support these missions. C-47s would fly wounded between transit hospitals on evacuation routes.

On longer routes, ATC and NATS were, from early 1944, coordinated by the Joint Army-Navy Transport Committee under the Joint Chiefs of Staff, even though each remained operationally a single service. Throughout the war, ATC and NATS continued to use ex-airline staff under contract, although these were increasingly replaced by military personnel. By the end of the war, ATC relied on airline personnel for only 19 per cent of its air transport missions, as opposed to 88 per cent in 1942.

In 1944 ATC expanded its routes to major Pacific bases, allowing the numbered air forces to concentrate their hard-worked C-47 units in support of combat operations. In May, 15 C-47s from ATC's South Pacific Wing were based at Guadalcanal, maintaining the links with Espiritu Santo and New Caledonia. ATC's Southwest Pacific Operations were reinforced with 100 C-47s in May-August, as it extended the New Guinea terminal of its service from Port Moresby to Nadzab (June) and Hollandia (September) by moving aircraft up to the main bomber bases in these areeas.

By mid-1944, new-production C-47s were being delivered with an improved, lightweight Fairchild-designed litter support system that allowed up to 24 litter patients to be carried per aircraft, rather than 18 as had previously been the case with the Douglas system. Many of these were used by ATC as they increasingly took over the casualty evacuation mission. ATC also established dedicated search and rescue detachments along its routes, many of which flew C-47s.

NATS, focused on its transport mission, remained the primary US Navy operator of R4Ds in the Pacific. And with more and more R4Ds becoming available in 1944, NATS proved able to meet the greater logistical challenge imposed by operating massive naval fleets from forward bases in the western Pacific. As the size of the fleet increased, so did the need for air logistical support, with units flying additional missions such as airlifting the fleet's mail and fresh food to Ulithi and other forward bases, in addition to bringing in priority cargo and personnel. The traffic in the other direction was not neglected either, with NATS forming specialised air evacuation squadron VRE-1.

By 1944, the increased number of C-47/R4Ds allowed USAAF service groups and depots to acquire a handful of C-47s to deliver high priority cargo such as aircraft engines. Many fighter and bomber units also acquired – often by rebuilding war-weary transports – their own C-47/R4Ds, which they kept busy carrying mail, food, cargo and leave parties. The Navy also issued R4Ds to a number of units outside NATS, with the Coast Guard, for example, putting modified aircraft into service to conduct search and rescue missions along the US west coast.

With more C-47/R4Ds now available, both the USAAF and US Navy followed ATC's lead by forming search and rescue squadrons. C-47s with specialist crews carried out visual search and supply drops to downed crews – missions that transport aircraft had carried out on an emergency basis throughout the war – as well as participating in occasional air rescues. In one instance, following a crash in a remote valley in New Guinea, a 374th TCG C-47 was used to fly in a CG-4A glider with medical personnel and equipment to allow the survivors to be successfully snatched up in the glider by an airborne C-47.

The 1944 advance through western New Guinea and onto the Philippines further increased the number of overwater flights made by Allied aircraft in-theatre, and C-47A 'X535' of the 21st TCS was involved in the rescue of two aircrew whose aircraft came down during this period. 'X535's' pilot, Capt William H Davis, gave the following account of the rescue, his aircraft being crewed by 2Lt Lawrence (co-pilot), 2Lt Schafer (navigator), TSgt Covington (engineer) and Sgt Godwin (radio);

'At 0705 hrs on 12 November 1944, C-47A "X535" took off from Peleliu for Biak. After climbing to 12,200 ft, we levelled off and started a very gradual descent, flying slightly east of our course in order to avoid some high build-ups of cumulus clouds. At 0910 hrs our navigator sighted a flash directly ahead and to the right side of our aeroplane. By this time we had let down to 11,500 ft.

'We peeled off and circled down to the water, where we spotted a single life raft with only one man waving at us. We called Biak on our liaison radio, gave our approximate position and turned on our IFF emergency signal. Noemfoor and Biak were both unable to get a bearing on us. We kicked out a life-raft, which spilled its sea marker fluid when it hit, about 150 ft from the other raft. In our third buzz of the raft, we saw a second man rise up from the bottom of it .

'At 1020 hrs we sighted a PBY – "Daylight 30" – due west of us. We were circling the raft at 600 ft. Rainstorms were closing in all around us and visibility got very low. The PBY was unable to find us even though we told him which direction to fly towards us. The PBY was unable to take a bearing on us because practically all of his radio equipment was out. His radar was not working at all. We kept approximate locations of each other by the build and fade of our radio liaison transmitter on each aeroplane.

'At approximately 1130 hrs we again sighted the PBY to the northwest. After telling him where we were, again we lost sight of the raft because a large thunder and rainstorm moved over it. We were unable to fly into it because of the terrific rain and turbulent air. The PBY reached us and we both circled the storm for approximately 80 minutes before we again sighted the raft on the south side of the rain storm. We buzzed the raft so that the PBY would see it, and then circled while the PBY landed and picked up the two men.'

This one-off two-tone C-47 was photographed on 'Cub 13' strip in the Russell Islands in August 1944. The mix of natural metal and camouflaged sections suggests that the aircraft has been partially stripped down to natural metal to reflect the fact that, by this time, the Russell Islands were a rear area. However, outside of ATC and NATS, and aircraft rebuilt in-theatre, natural metal C-47/R4Ds were a rare sight in the Pacific (*National Archives*)

NEW GUINEA AND THE PHILIPPINES 1944-45

The Allied advance across western New Guinea in 1944 followed the pattern set in the previous years' campaign, with Fifth Air Force C-47s (with RAAF Dakotas integrated into their operations) used to make possible the liberation of the Hollandia and Aitape areas. Engineers leapfrogged forward by air following amphibious invasions to restore or create airstrips and ports that would help the next advance towards the Philippines. As was often the case in the South and South West Pacific Areas, C-47s had to be supplemented by bombers pulled away from their primary missions to act as transports, or to ferry their own ground echelons to new bases.

Proposals for a purely airborne invasion of Selaroe Island, off New Guinea, in the summer 1944 were ultimately turned down by Gen MacArthur's headquarters. Instead, on 3-4 July 1944, C-47s of the

A C-47 of the 374th TCG is hauled off soft ground back onto an airstrip in New Guinea by Papuan muscle-power (*National Archives*)

55th TCS C-47 *Texas Honey* was the first transport aircraft to fly into Hollandia's Cyclops airfield. The aircraft was crewed on this mission, flown from Nadzab, by Col A J Beck (Assistant A-3 of the Fifth Air Force), who was the pilot, and co-pilot Capt Chuck Beck (433rd TCG HQ). Its landing was a particularly dramatic one, as the C-47 had to be pulled up so short on the bomb-damaged runway that the crew thought the landing gear might come through the nacelles – the pilot swerved around two bomb craters in his truncated roll out. The next day, after the aircraft had been inspected and repairs made to the runway, the *Texas Honey* flew back to Nadzab with 23 wounded aboard. It is seen here at Cyclops taxiing past the wreck of an 'Oscar II' on 28 April 1944 (*National Archives*)

A view from the DZ of 317th TCG C-47s dropping paratroops of the 503rd PIR on Noemfoor in what was only the second American airborne assault of the war. This photograph was taken on the second day of the airdrop (4 July 1944) when, as is apparent from the construction equipment, the hastily built coral airstrip on the island was almost complete – its hard surface led to many drop casualties among the paratroopers. By this time Japanese opposition had been reduced to sporadic sniper fire (*National Archives*)

Hollandia-based 317th TCG dropped 1500 troops of the 503rd PIR on Kamiri airstrip on the island of Noemfoor, near Biak, off the west coast of New Guinea. Unlike the Nadzab assault, the DZ was already in US hands, with paratroopers being committed as reinforcements rather than assault troops. A smokescreen covering the paratroopers from sniper fire on the second day of the drop shrouded the airstrip DZ, leading to many jump casualties.

Transports were also committed to building up air power in western New Guinea as preparations for the next campaigns were made. USAAF and Marine Corps transports were first in to airstrips in the Palaus and Peleliu (from the Central Pacific Area) and Morotai, as the Allies edged ever closer to the Philippines.

C-47A-30-DL 42-23582 *HONEYMOON EXPRESS* of the 374th TCG's 41st TCS provides the backdrop for this photograph, taken at Hollandia on 3 July 1944. Previously the lead aeroplane for the Nadzab airdrop, as well as several other key operations, it is shown here with squadron aircrew after flying as lead ship on the Noemfoor operation. The personnel in this shot include the aircraft's pilot on the Noemfoor drop, Maj Herbert Waldman (wearing a '50-mission crush' cap in the centre of the back row) from the 317th TCG HQ, who, as with most of the other aircrew, was also a veteran of the Nadzab drop (*National Archives*)

Paratroopers of the 503rd PIR wait patiently in their C-47 as the transport heads for the DZ at Noemfoor (*National Archives*)

More transports arrived as the USAAF's ETO needs abated – C-46s, as well as the more numerous C-47s. With 2842 C-47s delivered by Douglas in the first half of 1944 alone, the USAAF could begin to return impressed DC-3s – and contract crews flying for ATC – back to the airlines. It had been decided that as many C-47/R4D units in the Pacific theatres as possible would re-equip with C-46s. However, the C-47 could operate from airfields that were too small for the Curtiss transport, as well as drop supplies where the bigger aircraft – vulnerable to in-flight fire from battle damage – could not manoeuvre. The more complex and less reliable C-46 also strained maintenance resources.

Many units, therefore, retained some C-47s, while a number of C-46 squadrons also acquired one or more C-47s to allow them to operate into unprepared strips. The 403rd TCG was typical in its aircrews' reaction to news that the unit was to convert to C-46s;

'It has been more or less intimated that all C-47s will have been replaced by C-46s no later than 1 August 1945. The prospect has been met with varying degrees of enthusiasm by the flight crews. Initial opposition was emphatic. It is understandable that flight personnel reject what is to them an unproven aircraft in favour of one they know from personal experience to have proved its efficiency. In almost two years as overwater combat flying pilots, they have learned to substitute the C-47 for a dog as man's best friend. Too many pilots have successfully crash-landed C-47s or nursed them home on a single engine in instrument weather to get hilariously enthusiastic overnight about an "unknown quantity" replacement. Add to that the comparatively poor combat record of the C-46 since its arrival in the theatre, and their distrust is understandable.'

C-47 crews in New Guinea had also started to reap the benefits from improved technology installed in their aircraft during 1944. The SCR-729/APN-2 Rebecca (airborne) and Eureka (ground

C-47As prepare for loading at an unidentified airfield on the northern coast of New Guinea in mid-1944. The aircraft in the foreground, 42-24262, was lost in a combat accident on 30 June 1944, but the adjacent aircraft, 42-24263, survived the war only to be scrapped in the Philippines in 1945 (National Archives)

41st TCS C-47A 42-100721 The HIAWATHA wore DAT marking VH-CFQ on its tail instead of a serial when photographed in New Guinea in early 1944 – aircraft number '51' has also been painted forward of the transport's cargo doors. A short while after this shot was taken, DAT ordered that aircraft numbers be applied on the nose as well. Part of the original equipment of the 41st TCS 'Flying Trainmen', 42-100721 was also scrapped in the Philippines post-war, but not until April 1948 (Author's Collection)

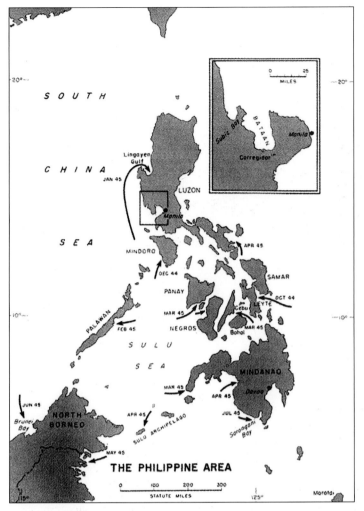

A US Army map of the Philippines Area, with arrows marking various offensives (box shows details of the fortress island of Corregidor, in Manila Bay) (*US Army*)

Brig Gen Warren Carter (shown here with a C-54) commanded the 54th TCW between May and November 1944. On either side of Carter's spell as CO, the wing had been led by Brig Gen Paul Prentiss, who had flown the lead ship (the 41st TCS's *HONEYMOON EXPRESS*) during the Nadzab parachute assault. Carter's main task was preparation for the liberation of the Philippines, which meant working with FEAF to leave behind their bases in New Guinea and the Solomons, painstakingly built up in 1943-44, for new ones that would be springboards for the invasion (*National Archives*)

station) radio beacon systems were widespread, these being used to help identify drop zones for supplies. APN-4 LORAN radio navigation sets appeared in 1945. Finally, C-47Bs, with R-1830-90 engines fitted with superchargers and extra fuel capacity to allow them to fly the 'Hump', entered production in 1944. Improved internal cargo-handling equipment, including powered conveyors, joined the improvised rollers and slides that had entered service in 1943. However, throughout the Pacific and CBI, muscle power of 'pushers and kickers' still made airdrops possible.

More specialised medical air evacuation units were deployed too, with the 54th TCW alone having three by mid-1944. Without aircraft of their own, these squadrons provided medical personnel – including flight nurses – for C-47s and R4Ds of all organisations.

The linking of the Fifth and Thirteenth Air Forces under Far East Air Forces (Provisional) HQ in June 1944 was intended to centralise US air power for the Philippines campaign (DAT was disbanded in October 1944).

Arnold and USAAF HQ in Washington DC proposed using transport aircraft in an enlarged version of Wingate's vision to begin the campaign with an airborne invasion of Mindanao in September 1944 – 650 C-47s and 735 gliders seizing a base, with the 11th Airborne Division (newly arrived in the theatre) then invading the other islands, first Leyte and then Luzon, with airborne forces supported by amphibious landings. This would have required extensive reinforcement from the US, for although the FEAF had 460 transports – mainly C-47s – these were all heavily committed even without an airborne invasion. MacArthur instead decided for an amphibious invasion of Leyte.

C-47s moved into airfields on Leyte in October 1944, soon after the invasion. The New Guinea

CHAPTER FIVE

The pilot of C-47A 43-16119 *Classy Chassis* from the 317th TCG waves to local Filipinos at Hill Field, Mindoro, in December 1944. This aircraft later took part in the parachute assault on Camalaniugua (*National Archives*)

pattern of seizing an intermediate airstrip – here before the invasion of the main island of Luzon – led to the invasion of Mindoro in December. Again a proposal for an air invasion was turned down by MacArthur, but when weather interrupted over-the-beach re-supply, transports flew in 600 barrels of aviation fuel a day to the fighter strips – daylight missions

A war-weary C-47 flies over the ruins of Manila whilst conducting a DDT spraying mission (*National Archives*)

were often flown with fighter escort. Between 29 November and 5 December, 250 paratroopers were dropped over a tiny DZ – one C-47 made 14 passes – at Manarawat, on Leyte, delivering reinforcements to ground troops.

The invasion of Luzon opened in January 1945, by which point special operations had become an important FEAF C-47 mission, with airdrops to guerrilla units and participation in raids to liberate prisoners. C-47s also provided humanitarian relief to a cut-off leper colony and, when a malaria epidemic threatened Manila, conducted large-scale air spraying.

Of course most missions involved critical airdrops for advancing ground forces. On 22 January, Capt Kelly of the 39th TCS co-piloted C-47 'X31' for the 40th TCS. He later reported;

'Pilot Capt Tully and navigator Lt Stinchfield, both from the 39th, and crew chief and radio operator from the 40th. Nine aeroplanes took off for drop missions to Luzon at targets "B" and "C", flying formations in "V of Vs". Target "B" located at 122°31'E, 13°37'N. Target "C" located at 122°50'E, 13°39'N. All aeroplanes headed for target "B". Capt Tully, flight leader, led five aeroplanes to target "C", where they made drops. The other four dropped at target "B". When drops were completed, all nine aeroplanes joined in formation and returned together. At "C" target, aeroplane "X31" made three free drops at 50 ft, and four paratroops at 200 ft. Seven runs were made over the target. Over target 30 minutes. Target was marked by three hills in a triangular position with smoke on them. 100 per cent accuracy. However, one bundle paradrop missed target. Do not know which aeroplane dropped it. Course at drop was 125°. Very rough terrain, rolling hills.

'At "C" target there were Filipinos and GIs on ground – one, a major, was recognised by an infantry second lieuteneant in our aeroplane. Cargo was demolition equipment, gas and food. Weather was good throughout, except light rain in

The 3rd ACG was deployed to the Philippines in an effort to try and repeat the CBI tactics used so successfully by the Chindits. However, the group simply ended up being integrated into the overall C-47 transport force in this more established theatre, dominated by Gen MacArthur's unitary command structure. *CHARLOTTE M* served with the 3rd ACG's 318th TCS(C) on Luzon in May 1945. As with the other ACGs, the 3rd was proud of its group insignia (white fin top). The 318th's aircraft names were all painted on 'cloud' backgrounds. The 'A' prefix to the aircraft's number was part of an attempt to standardise such markings within the FEAF (*National Archives*)

What the ground forces saw most often – a C-47 coming off a DZ, here in the Philippines in 1945 (*National Archives*)

The fortress island of Corregidor in Manila Bay, as seen from one of the 317th TCG aircraft taking part in the parachute assault on 16 February 1945. US Navy patrol boats can just be seen offshore, these vessels playing a vital role in rescuing paratroopers that missed not only the narrow DZs, but the entire island (*National Archives*)

The USAAF's TCSs were well-trained in formation flying as part of their primary mission. As if to prove the point, here a vee-formation of C-47s of the 317th TCG head for Corregidor on 16 February 1945. As the aircraft approached the DZ, however, they would shift into a line-astern formation so that only one aircraft would be over the DZ at a time (*National Archives*)

Samar Sea en route to Luzon. Trip took from four to four-and-a-half hours (round trip). However, waited two to three hours in air for fighter cover, so aeroplanes were airborne 7 hours 25 minutes. Had two-aeroplane fighter cover. Started with four, but two turned back because of bad weather.'

The opening stages of the Luzon campaign included the largest parachute assault of the Pacific War. On 3 February, the 317th TCG's 48 C-47s dropped a total of three battalions of the 11th Airborne Division's 511th PIR on Tagaytay Ridge, encountering minimal resistance, but leading to a scattered and dispersed drop despite being in daylight. This was followed by a 51-aircraft mission later that day, which was also a dispersed drop. A follow-up mission the next day with 33 C-47s was, however, highly accurate.

Other C-47/R4D operators also took part in the Philippines campaign, NATS R4Ds joining in a massive airlift of replacement equipment after US Navy vessels suffered typhoon damage. Marine Corps R4Ds operated in the Philippines, acting as pathfinders for single-engined aircraft as they deployed. And while SCAT headquarters was disbanded in early 1945 – ATC and NATS taking over its routes – MAG-25 stayed in action. After the invasion of Luzon, ATC, anxious to make the Fifth Air Force transport veterans forget their 1942 jibes, beat the troop carrier units into many forward airfields and set up its Manila terminal whilst Japanese resistance was still being cleared out.

On 16 February 1945, 51 C-47s of the 317th TCG, nicknamed the 'Jungle Skippers', dropped 2000 men of the 503rd PIR on the fortress island of Corregidor, in Manila Bay. This was the one parachute assault of the Pacific War that led to a hard-fought battle, with the paratroopers being dropped on the two tiny DZs in daylight in the wake of a bombing strike to suppress anti-aircraft fire. Due to the modest size of the DZs, only one battalion could be dropped at a time, with a five-hour turn

around between drops. Each C-47 had to make repeated passes over the DZs, as only a handful of paratroopers could jump on each pass. Fighter escorts attacked the source of any ground fire.

The commanding officers of the 317th TCG and 503rd PIR – Lt Col John Lackey Jr and Col George Jones – circled the island in a C-47 command ship, directing each aircraft to the DZ. The 317th performed both drops, followed by re-supply missions the following day, without loss, although most of its C-47s received flak damage.

Exactly one week later, a well-planned raid on the internment camp at Los Banos, on Luzon, successfully liberated Allied prisoners just days before their planned execution by the Japanese. A company of 11th Airborne Division paratroopers dropped by ten C-47s – mostly from 65th TCS – seized the camp, routed the garrison and then linked up with guerrillas and a larger force of paratroopers that had landed from amphibious tractors, withdrawing with them and the surviving PoWs.

In addition to the normally high wartime risk of fratricide, the fact that the Japanese operated a practically identical aircraft to the C-47 in the L2D (Type 00) 'Tabby' transport further compounded the situation. On 10 February, the crew of C-47A 43-30761 of the 39th TCS was lost and about to make the fatal error of landing on a Japanese-held island when it was shot down, on final approach to the island's runway, by a P-51. In what was the war's only friendly fire incident that actually saved lives, the Mustang pilot received credit for an aerial kill – he had a blue-and-white star painted beneath his cockpit! Upon their return to base, this is the story the C-47 crew told the squadron intelligence officer for the record;

'C-47A "X-23" of the 39th TCS left Leyte at 0700 hrs on 10 February 1945. There were eight passengers aboard ship, two of whom were nurses. Our destination was Clark Field. We were not flying formation, nor following any other ship. On take-off, the aeroplane had 650 gallons of fuel. Flew to Hill Field at 10,000 ft. At 0915 hrs we were over Hill Field. The aeroplane then flew along the west coast of Mindoro on a course of 340°, crossing the northwest part of Mindoro at about 120°50'E so as to avoid a mountain which was 3000-4000 ft high. The C-47 continued north. When it was on the south side of Manila Bay, it was 1100 hrs.

'At the southern edge of Manila Bay, the aeroplane encountered broken, scattered clouds. It climbed to 7000 ft and flew through rough weather until 1130 hrs, bucking a strong head wind. It was still over water. At 1150 hrs the pilot instructed the radio operator to ask for a bearing and send an SOS. IFF emergency was turned on, and remained on continuously until we ditched. The radio operator talked in the clear on command and liaison (radio networks). The pilot and co-pilot did not speak on the radio. We received no bearings or response of any kind.

317th TCG CO Lt Col John Lackey briefs crews at Nipa, Luzon, on 23 June 1945 – the eve of the parachute assault on Camalaniugua. As a captain, and commanding officer of the 6th TCS, he led the first formation flight of 13 C-47s from California to Port Moresby in October 1942. The various route maps giving details of the impending mission have been taped onto the fuselage of C-47B 43-49757, which survived the operation and went on to serve with the occupation forces in Japan. The aircraft was finally withdrawn from use in 1947 (*National Archives*)

Veteran C-53 41-20054 VH-CCC
"YOUHADDABUCK" had initially
arrived in Brisbane in 1942 and
went on to serve with the RAAF
as VH-CCC. It was transferred to
Qantas control two years later,
before being returned to the USAAF
in April 1944. The aircraft remained
in US military service until 1947,
when it appeared on the Philippine
civil register. Eventually sold to a
US buyer, the C-53 ended up flying
with the Colombian Air Force until
written off in a crash at Cali on
3 August 1981 (*Author's Collection,
photo by TSgt Walter D Kudler*)

'The aeroplane continued until 1150 hrs, and was still over water. The pilot then informed his passengers that he was in trouble and would set the aeroplane down on the first land he saw. Safety belts were put on the seats, life-jackets put on – rafts were prepared, with food, water, guns and ammo laid out ready to be put into the rafts. The door was removed. The pilot, Lt Grieger, took a heading due east and flew until 1210 hrs, when two small isles were observed to the south a few miles.

'We flew past the two small isles on a heading of 90° for 20 minutes, and then saw no more land. We made a 180° banked turn, due west at 270° to the same two small isles. The aeroplane was just above the overcast at 4000 ft. Overcast was broken. The two isles we saw were too small to land on. We saw and flew to a longer isle. Its terrain was too rough. We saw a still longer isle, approached it and saw an airstrip of grass about 3500 ft x 100 ft, but no tower or buildings. The strip was at the eastern edge of a town. The isle was about three-quarters of a mile across. We were definitely lost.

'The gear was put down, and at 150 ft altitude, with the aeroplane at half flaps and about to be put down, six strings of tracers came up in front of us. The pilot thought it was Japanese ground fire, and was in line with the approaching strip. He turned the aeroplane slightly to the right, then made a sharp turn to the left, getting down as low as possible towards the ocean.

'A P-51 made a head on pass at and over the C-47, striking the C-47 in the right engine and fuselage with several shots. Then the C-47 continued in a direct line for the shore. When he reached it, the P-51 made a pass from the rear, shooting into the fuselage and left engine of the C-47. The functioning of our motors was not impaired by the gun fire we received. We ditched 300 yards from shore, at 65 to 70 mph airspeed in a complete stall, all switches off – the tail was dropped on a smooth sea. The fuselage settled and the right wing dropped, causing the aeroplane to swerve to the right. This was at 1400 hrs. The C-47 travelled roughly 50-70 ft on the surface. It stayed afloat for three to five minutes.

'We took two minutes to get out. We did not rush, as the aeroplane was not filling with water. No one lost their heads. Baggage for the passengers, three tool chests and two bags of mail had been thrown out of the door. A trailer weighing about 1500 lbs was still in the aeroplane. Four rafts were put out. One was perforated by bullets and sank. The 12 of us got into the three rafts. The P-51 circled us for an hour but did not fire again.

'I ordered all rafts to paddle out to sea as fast as possible. We were out about a mile when machine guns and rifles opened up on us from the shore. We were out of range, but the shooting continued for 30 minutes. We found ourselves in the centre of a triangle composed of two smaller isles and the one we had tried to land on, so we stayed equidistant from them all and waited until dark. None of us were injured, except one person had a minor cut and one a hole in his shoe, with part of his large toe-nail missing. At dusk we put to sea between the two small isles, put up our sails and rowed for five or six miles against a strong current.

The parachute assault at Camalaniugua on 23 June 1945 was conducted in daylight by the 317th TCG. The aircraft closest to the camera is *CleoC* of the 39th TCS, which was part of the second flight of the 317th over the DZ (*National Archives*)

C-47s *Angel in Blue* and *The Sioux* of the 33rd TCS were photographed on the flightline at Palau on 16 June 1945 (*National Archives*)

'Weather was good at all times. At night, we were cold in our suntans (khaki cotton uniforms), having taken no blankets aboard. One of our three rafts started to deflate at 0100 hrs on 11 February. Continuous pumping kept it quite full.

'At daylight, the waves were so high they broke into our rafts. Also, very large timbers were being thrown about. We pushed them off with our paddles. So, we went back between the three isles, in the lee of one of them. None of us was hungry or thirsty until 1000 hrs on the 11th when we ate and drank sparingly.

'At 1045 hrs a P-51 pilot joined us on a raft. He stated he was the wingman of the P-51 that shot us down, and that he parachuted out when his aeroplane was hit by Japanese ground fire 30 minutes before we were hit. At 1100 hrs we were picked up by a Catalina. Later, we found we had ditched in Songsong Bay, west of Batan Island, midway between Luzon and Formosa.'

Aside from carrying freight and troops, the 317th TCG was also called upon to perform bombing missions with its C-47s against pockets of Japanese resistance on islands in Manila Bay. Capt Max W Custer, veteran C-47 pilot and operations officer of the 317th TCG, reported;

'On 12 April the first bombing mission by troop carrier aeroplanes in this theatre of operations was carried out by C-47s of the "Jungle Skippers". The target, Carabao Island, is located on the south side of the south channel to the entrance of Manila Bay. This island lies about half-a-mile from the mainland, north of Limbones Cove. It is about 1200 yards long, not more than 200 yards wide and 185 ft high. The shore is mainly composed of sheer cliff, in places 100 ft high. Intelligence reports indicated that 800 enemy troops were hiding on the island.

'Two aeroplanes made two missions, each dropping a total of 48 x 55 gallons of napalm. The aeroplanes flew at extremely low altitude, with drums being pushed out of the cargo door when signalled by the pilot. The entire island was covered. Two-thirds of the drums spread upon contact and burned fiercely, and the remaining one-third exploded in a concentrated puff where they hit without any spread. Time over the target was limited and aeroplanes had to return without having observed the results of their bombing runs. The island was left aflame and the wooden buildings near the southern end were destroyed.

'On 15 April another aeroplane made one mission on the same target, dropping 12 x 55 gallons of napalm. Its purpose was to hit spots on the island covered by brush. One explosion was started on the southwest end of the island. The missions were considered successful, and higher commands were well pleased with the results.'

However, the vast majority of transport missions throughout the Philippines followed the pattern set in New Guinea – airdrops to combat troops, casualty evacuation and priority cargo to enable aircraft to operate from new bases.

C-47 'X33' of the 'Jungle Skippers' flies in formation with other 317th TCG aircraft on 23 June 1945, en route to Camalaniugua (*National Archives*)

As C-46 numbers increased, C-47s were concentrated on casualty evacuation, special operations, parachute assaults and frontline re-supply missions. The latter remained highly challenging, as reported by 1Lt Frank Fisher Jr of the 65th TCS, who was sent to re-supply elements of the US 6th Infantry Division in the rocky Cayayuan Valley;

'On 26 July we left Dulag and flew to Lingayen strip, where Capt Neil Mulford of Group Headquarters directed that we drop in the Banahue area to 6th Division men. We spent five days flying out of there, dropping to the troops. Each morning we would pick up drop crews and an officer from the infantry to guide us to the drop zone. Upon completion, we were complimented upon the percentage of recoveries made of material dropped – 85 per cent recovery was made, which was much superior, we were told, to the outfit that had previously been doing the job.

'Thirteen different loads were taken by my ship into the drop area, and once for a series of 12 consecutive drops we made a "hit" every time. We were dropping rations by free drop, and medical supplies, including plasma, by parachute. The difficulties encountered were mainly that the terrain features offered hazards. Drops were made as low as possible (about 200 ft above ground). Altitude gained – within two miles – had to be 2500 ft so as to clear the mountains. We would go into the valley, drop wheels and flaps, throttle back to 110 mph, drop, pull up the wheels, push the throttle to the panel and sweat. Part of the pattern was flown over the Japanese positions, but they offered no threats.'

The 317th TCG, experienced in parachute assaults, as well as the daily air re-supply and casualty evacuation, was linked with elements of the 511th PIR as the Gypsy Task Force. On 23 June 1945, at Apari, on northern Luzon, this force (plus eight 433rd TCG C-46s towing gliders) made the last airborne assault of the Pacific War, dropping paratroops on an airstrip help by guerrillas.

With the defeat of major Japanese forces and the extension of ATC and NATS routes, FEAF concentrated most of its C-47 squadrons north of Okinawa, in preparation for the invasion of Japan. Others units remained committed to the continuing campaign in the southern Philippines.

CBI 1945

Supply drops to frontline troops made the 1945 offensive that liberated Burma possible. Indeed, the campaign in the northern part of the country was almost totally dependent on air transport. The sheer scale of the airdrops required is shown by the fact that, starting in late 1944, between 50,000 and 80,000 parachutes were expended a month by the USAAF over Burma, with an additional ten per cent used over China (and many cargos, especially food, were dropped without parachutes). These numbers declined in 1945 as more forward airstrips were built in Burma.

Troops were flown in as soon as strips were secure to keep the advance going. Furthermore, the building of a road and petroleum pipeline from Ledo, in India, through northern Burma to China required additional airlift support, with C-47s flying sections of pipe into Chinese airfields.

The CCTF's 16 transport squadrons – USAAF, RAF and RCAF – supported the campaign in southern Burma. On 19 February, loaded gliders were ferried by C-47s to the forward field at Sinthe. However, the airstrip at Thabuktan was captured intact and, preceded by a single glider containing air traffic control, C-47s started bringing in Indian troops on 27 February. In March, during a month of intensive combat, 70,000 tons were airlifted to the forces on the Burma front and 26,000 tons to troops in the north. Finally, C-47s of the 1st and 2nd ACGs flew an Indian Army brigade into Meiktila to cut off the Japanese retreat route from Mandalay.

Meiktila was itself in the frontline, with landings and take-offs often coming under fire from nearby Japanese artillery positions. On 15 March, at the height of the battle for nearby Mandalay, 1Lt Wayne Bishop was flying C-47 '824' of the 317th TCS;

'I entered the traffic pattern at Meiktila at about 1715 hrs. On the downwind leg, close to the field, we observed bursts about the runway and in the unloading area. The tower advised "Land. Taxi to the south end, kick 'em out and get the hell out of here. Do not cut engines".

'Turning on the base leg, close in, we saw puffs in the north-east which prompted me to get down to the runway quickly. Approaching the end of the runway, we observed a fresh burst midway down the run-way. We raised the gear and buzzed the runway to investigate the dam-age. No damage. I pulled up, made another close pattern and landed. Holding the tail up, I taxied fast to the south end, where there appeared to be a few bursts. But at the south

Representing the high degree of coordination achieved by 1945 in the CBI, a C-47 drops supplies at the crossing of the Irrawaddy River in February 1945 while a British-air-ground control party, mounted in a jeep and a tank, direct both frontline re-supply and tactical air support. In Burma, tactical air support meant a lot more than just fighters and bombers attacking enemy positions. Transport aircraft performed missions that were just as vital to the troops in the field, keeping them re-supplied with everything from 'bullets to baked beans', and conducting crucial casualty evacuation missions. 'Never, I believe, was air cooperation closer, quicker, or more effective; never was it more gratefully appreciated than by the Fourteenth Army and its commander' was how the British Army's Gen William Slim viewed the operations around the Irrawaddy River in February 1945 (*National Archives*)

Capt Culp of CCTF briefs C-47 crews on Operation *Dracula* – the airborne assault on Rangoon on 1 May 1945. This mission was a truly Allied effort, with US aircraft and crews, RCAF jumpmasters and British signallers jumping with the Gurkha paratroopers (*National Archives*)

The remains of a burnt-out C-47 from the 2nd ACG litter Meiktila airfield in March 1945. The fly-in and re-supply efforts at this strategically critical airfield were often subjected to Japanese artillery fire (*National Archives*)

end we caught an explosion under the tail which threw all personnel in the rear to the floor. I thought a tyre might have been hit. The aeroplane following observed what they thought was a ground loop. The tower shouted "'35', are you okay?" We were obscured by smoke.

'We unloaded the aeroplane in nothing flat. The crew chief, upon inspection, found no damage, and we taxied fast to take-off from the runway. The tower then advised as a shell hit the runway, "Caution on take-off '35'. Large shell holes in runway".

'I threw on 48 inches of mercury, lifted the tail, lowered half flaps and was off the ground at 65 mph before reaching the holes in the runway. I banked sharply to the left back over the village and climbed out of danger.

'Close examination upon landing at Palel showed one dent in the right elevator about the size of a mess kit. We believe this was caused by concussion from the blast. A smaller dent in the same elevator appeared to be shrapnel. No further damage was found.'

The Allies hoped to take Rangoon prior to the onset of the monsoon season, and on 30 April some 39 C-47s from the 1st and 2nd ACGs and the 1st CCG dropped 800 Gurkha paratroopers near the city as part of Operation *Dracula*. The drop was coordinated with an amphibious invasion, and Allied troops encountered precious little resistance when they took Rangoon several days later. This was a highly successful parachute assault, as the 317th TCS's report shows;

'At 0230 hrs on 1 May, Pathfinder aeroplane "645" of the 317th TCS(C) and aeroplane "840" of the CCTF took off, with 20 paratroopers in "645" and two Visual Control Point Groups, consisting of 20 men, in "840". Col McCullough of the CCTF was the pilot of "645" and Capt Richard Braswell, of the 317th TCS(C), his co-pilot.

'At 0300 hrs, Maj Neil Holm took off with the lead aeroplane. Shortly thereafter, 39 319th and 317th TCS and CCTF aeroplanes were airborne. The mission was on its way as scheduled.

'The weather at Akyab on take-off was not encouraging. There was overcast at 3000 ft and distant lightning. By the time all aeroplanes were airborne, a thunderstorm was passing the stations with heavy rains. The rains turned into a steady drizzle, which continued until 0730 hrs.

'The course was Akyab-Myingui-Kyuin-Payagyi-DZ. Aeroplanes "645" and "840" were over the DZ at 0545 hrs. They dropped their men without incident. Three P-51s gave them escort from the IP to the DZ. No signs of enemy action were observed, except for a few wooden barges making for the shore in the Rangoon River.

'The formation of the 319th TCS(C) aeroplanes, led by Maj Holm, dropped their paratroopers about 40 minutes later. The 317th TCS(C), led by Maj Richard Edwards reached the DZ at 0633 hrs. All paratroopers and parapacks were dropped in a small circle on the DZ. Returning pilots reported the escorting P-51s. The weather at the DZ was overcast at 1500 ft. Another larger overcast was at 3000 ft, although visibility remained good.

'All of the aeroplanes returned to Akyab successfully except for "246", which landed on Ramree Island due to engine trouble. This aeroplane arrived at Akyab about two hours later. The mission can be considered as a highly successful one, as no aeroplanes were damaged and no personnel injured. Forty-one C-47s carried 820 and dropped them successfully.'

A series of Japanese ground offensives against US air bases in China were launched between April 1944 and February 1945, and these led to a crisis use of air transport in-theatre. Despite the Fourteenth Air Force's air superiority, it was unable to halt the advancing Japanese, moving by night and requiring minimal logistics. Although an additional airlift of fuel and ammunition over the 'Hump' was desperately needed in an effort to sustain the Fourteenth Air Force's effort, there were not enough transports available to provide it. As the Japanese reached their objectives, there were many last-minute air evacuations of forward bases.

To help stem the Japanese advance, Chinese troops were flown from Burma in a series of airlifts. In December 1944, the Tenth Air Force conducted Operation *Grubworm*, which saw 25,000 troops brought in from Burma to defend the now-threatened airlift terminal at Kunming. These flights provoked a major resurgence in Japanese aerial activity in the region, as 27th TCS pilot 1Lt Jack M Engle discovered;

'Some of the Zeros got one of our ships one day as he was climbing away from Target 55. Shot him down when he didn't have a ghost of a chance. They scared the hell out of a lot more of us too many different times. It became habitual to keep our heads moving in the cockpit, eyes searching the sky for single-engined aircraft. One man kept vigil in the navigator's dome, constantly alert for specks in the distance, and at those times, that man, regardless of who he was, was the most important person aboard the aircraft. All other lives on that ship depended on him.

Jettisonable parapacks of British design are fitted to temporary external hardpoints beneath a CCTF C-47 in preparation for Operation *Dracula* (*National Archives*)

'There were many false alarms, of course, when everything was "pushed to the firewall" and we made every effort to put ourselves some place else. But a dozen false alarms are better than once failing to see enemy aeroplanes. Nerves were on edge. We had no desire to dogfight a Zero in a C-47 – who does? But Zeros, ack-ack and the monsoons combined couldn't stop our aeroplanes from dropping supplies on the "Hump" every day.'

C-47s in China were required to re-supply frontline units as Japanese offensives continued. Others landed behind Japanese lines, inserting OSS and weather teams, or picking up downed US aircrews – the China-based 8th Emergency Rescue Squadron carried out many of the latter missions. Elsewhere in-theatre, C-47s of the 69th Composite Wing – supplemented by bombers – performed airdrops to beleaguered French forces retreating in Indochina. The 27th TCS war diary provides a few details;

'16 April – 1Lt McCleary (pilot), with 2Lt Mellon (co-pilot), 2Lt Robinson (navigator), Maj Bannon (observer), Sgt Weatherly (crew chief) and Sgt Korish (radio operator), undertook a drop mission to Pinfok, just a few miles from the Japanese base of Mon Cay, in French Indochina, and about ten miles from the Gulf of Tonkin. The mission was successful, and badly needed supplies were dropped to the French groups moving out of French Indochina.

'23 April – while landing at Poseh in C-47 "425", 1Lt Taylor had just touched down when a tyre blew out. The gear was drawn up and the aeroplane skidded to a stop without injury to the crew. The aeroplane was still repairable.

'25 April – a secret mission was flown to Szemao, where demolitions packed for dropping were loaded. Several paratroopers were taken on board. A mission was then flown over Indochina, where the men jumped and the demolitions were dropped. The crew on the mission were 1Lt Miller (pilot), 2Lt Mincher (co-pilot), Capt Quinliven (navigator), 2Lt Potts (navigator) (the two navigators suggests that this C-47 may have been a pathfinder with a modified SCR-711C H2X ground-mapping navigation radar), Cpl Gordon (crew chief) and SSgt Loughnane (radio operator).'

With the liberation of Burma and the disbandment of the EAC, the USAAF started to move most of the

Parachutes away – CCTF C-47s carry out the follow-up supply drop to Gurkha paratroops near Rangoon during Operation *Dracula* on 1 May 1945. The dark-coloured parachutes indicate that these are supplies being delivered rather than personnel. Jumpmasters for all drops on 1 May were provided by the RCAF (*National Archives*)

Tenth Air Force's C-47 strength into China, enabling the return of Chinese forces that had taken part in the Burma campaign. C-47s reinforced the 'Hump' airlift, eventually moving Tenth Air Force headquarters to Kunming. In May 1945, the 27th TCS moved to China to provide the same Chindit-style direct support to Chinese forces conducting an offensive along the Salween River, but operating by day rather than night, and with airdrops in place of missions into forward airstrips. 1Lt Jack Engle described the missions that his unit flew;

'The job assigned the 27th TCS was that of dropping food, ammunition, and other supplies to the Chinese troops trying to recapture the Burma Road. The actual country was new to us, but we were quite familiar with the type of terrain, and the task of dropping supplies. What it really consisted of was flying the "Hump" several times each day. Flying a drop pattern in mountains and valleys in the daytime certainly offered no problem when we had already done the same thing at night – in fact it was a relief.

'The slow and reluctant manner in which the Chinese fought and gradually gained ground, and the incessant red tape from their higher authorities, prolonged our supplying job far more than necessary. Many times we wished for the presence of some of our own efficient infantry, if only to show us that our efforts were helping to produce the desired results. But it was necessary to nip in the bud our typically American impatience, and do as we were ordered.

'We started with Target No 1, along the old muddy Salween River, and within a month our targets had increased in number to 25, stretching from north of Tengchung to south of Lungling. Some of them were in valleys, others on the sides or tops of mountains and hills. The country quickly became familiar to us, and we could find Tengchung, Chenanso, Lungling or Paoshan, or any spot on the Schweli, Salween or Mekong Rivers, as easily as we could find the corner drug store – not that western China knew what a drugstore was.

A precise 'V' of C-47s from the 317th TCS (with the 2nd ACG's exclamation mark insignia on their fins) drop Gurkha paratroopers near Rangoon as part of Operation *Dracula*. The C-47s carry British supply canisters under their bellies, and these were also dropped (*National Archives*)

Mule airlift to China from northern Burma by the 316th TCS on 1 February 1945. Note the five-band fuselage marking of the unit's parent 1st ACG (*National Archives*)

'And so it became a routine – Target 37 today, Alternate 49, or Target 60, Alternate 25, or some other combination. It wasn't bad, to us – dull, but not bad. All we had to worry about was the monsoon weather, with its constant changes and often impossible build-ups, or the turbulent air-currents in the tight little valleys in which we had to circle many times, very low, or the frequent ground fire from the fanatic little Nips.

'Then things began to change. The Jap became active, seemed to be awakening to the fact that we were flying over his ill-gotten territory every day. He realised that we were one of the major factors in a campaign that was not in accord with the Emperor's wishes, and he did not ignore the fact that we were flying unarmed ships at low altitudes.

'So he established an anti-aircraft emplacement on the west side of the Salween, where the Burma Road crosses the river – an ideal location, as we had to fly over it every day. We christened this ack-ack Jap "Dead-eye Dick". He did his job pretty efficiently. The gunners on "Dead-eye Dick's" hill gave several of us many bullet holes as souvenirs, and we had to alter our route around him.'

It was May 1945 before C-46s outnumbered the 501 C-47s then in the China and Burma-India theatres. 'Hump' tonnage continued to increase with the introduction of the Curtiss transport. The ability to fly the lower altitude routes over northern Burma and the investment in infrastructure in previous years by ATC was also now showing results. This included the use of centralised production line maintenance for transports, which achieved a readiness rate of 85 percent. By war's end ATC had 13 bases in India and six in China, and had delivered 740,000 tons to China – three-quarters of that in the last year of the war – in 167,285 sorties.

Some 167 C-47s were among the 700+ transports doing the job Gen Arnold had estimated would require 50-75 C-47s back in 1942. The cost had included 460 transports lost (seven shot down by the Japanese) and 792 personnel killed. At the peak of ATC operations, in August 1945, 1341 aircraft from its worldwide strength of 3090 transports were C-47 series machines.

A C-47 of the 27th TCS makes a low-level airdrop to Chinese forces on the Salween River front, dropping food without the use of parachutes (*National Archives*)

The end of the 'Hump' – base operations at the ATC terminal at Kunming, in China. Crews would report in on arrival and make arrangements for unloading their aircraft and picking up a backload, if available, for the return trip. The building of infrastructure, the provision of navigational aids and partial replacement of C-47s by C-46s and C-54s in the last year of the 'Hump's' operation were critical to its success (*Author's Collection*)

VICTORY 1944-46

The greater distances involved in the final stages of the conflict in the Pacific and CBI made the increasing numbers of longer-ranged C-46/R5Cs and C-54/R5Ds (largely limited to ATC and NATS) arriving in-theatre more important, but these were never numerous enough to totally supplant C-47/R4Ds.

High priority cargo moved by the latter during this period included highly explosive flamethrower fuel for the fighting on Saipan, Peleliu and other islands. In October 1944, when the Great Typhoon interrupted the unloading of supplies on Peleliu, the forces ashore were fed by an airlift.

Elsewhere, the forward fleet base established in Ulithi soon became a terminal for TAG and NATS transports. Indeed, at the height of US Navy operations at Ulithi, six R4Ds would arrive from Guam every morning with the fleet's mail, followed by more with its fresh food. TAG moved its routes forward, turning those in the rear areas over to NATS.

Air re-supply to frontline troops was also demonstrated to be vital even when there was no jungle terrain to deal with, as on Iwo Jima. Marine Corps R4Ds and R5Cs, as well as C-47s from the 9th TCS, made the first airdrops to Marines on the island on 28 February, and these were followed by extensive air re-supply and casualty evacuation missions. Some Marine Corps units had their mail airdropped to them too. As soon as the airfields were open on Iwo Jima, TAG transports acted as pathfinders for fighter units, as well as carrying in supplies and personnel for these groups. On Okinawa, C-47/R4Ds made airdrops to frontline

A crowd of Marine Corps personnel and US Navy Seabees meet C-47A 42-100799 on 24 October 1944. On that day it became the first C-47 to arrive at the airfield at Ulithi, in the Caroline Islands. This base was soon being heavily utilised in support of the Allied fleet in the western Pacific, with innumerable C-47s, R4Ds and RAF Dakotas (when the Royal Navy arrived for the Okinawa campaign in early 1945) bringing in personnel, priority supplies, mail and fresh food on inbound flights, and then leaving with combat casualties. This particular aircraft was salvaged in June 1945 following a landing accident (*National Archives*)

A Marine Corps R4D is loaded with wounded in preparation for a medical evacuation flight to Guam from Miyamoto field, Iwo Jima, in March 1945. Even after Marine Corps transport (previously utility) squadrons in the central Pacific had largely re-equipped with the R5C, the smaller R4D was preferred for short-range medevac flights because it was quicker to load and unload from ambulances. This in turn reduced the out-of-hospital time for wounded being evacuated up the chain (*National Archives*)

Low altitude DDT spraying missions were flown by C-47s and R4Ds followed the capture of Iwo Jima. Ground forces were highly appreciative of these sorties, which prevented the spread of diseases. The 9th TCS lost a C-47 and its crew to ground fire on one of these missions (*National Archives*)

troops, with their efforts supplemented by bomber units. And evacuation C-47/R4Ds were usually the first aeroplanes into island airfields as they became operational. Other missions included DDT spraying over malarial areas in the Marianas, Iwo Jima and Okinawa.

While the fighting was in progress in Okinawa, air transport facilities were set up to prepare for the invasion of Japan. With the campaign in the Philippines campaign coming to an end in the early summer of 1945, FEAF transports helped their forces deploy northwards. Planning for the invasion of Japan, FEAF units were then moved to Okinawa so as to be able to take part in the war's final offensive. The 11th Airborne Division and troop carrier units were to be ready for a parachute assault on an as-required basis, these battle-hardened squadrons being bolstered by additional transports and gliders brought in from the USA.

Following the capitulation of Japan, the 54th TCW planned and implemented Mission 75 – the airborne start of the Allied occupation. Starting on 28 August, 15 C-54s and 30 C-47s flew fuel and control parties into Atsugi airfield, near Tokyo. The main operation commenced on 30 August, when 180 C-54s (mainly ATC), 272 C-46s and 100 C-47s airlifted 12,000 troops of the 11th Airborne and 1st Cavalry Divisions to Japan, and evacuated 7500 newly released PoWs over the course of the following two weeks.

C-47s soon became part of the occupation, with the 55th TCS putting in place an improvised domestic air schedule, with airline-style titles that proclaimed them to be the 'Imperial Couriers'. In Korea, C-47s also were used to fly US forces throughout the southern part of the country.

In China, C-47s with OSS teams crisscrossed the country liberating PoWs and taking the surrender of Japanese garrisons. Most of the

C-47B-25-10 43-49023 *Traveler* was the personal aircraft of Maj Gen Robert B McClure, Commanding General, Chinese Combat Command. Not the least important role of the C-47 throughout the Pacific and CBI was providing mobility to flag officers, allowing them to effectively operate over large and geographically dispersed areas. Considering the distances involved, and the importance of logistics in these theatres, the C-47s were as vital to their users as the Fieseler Storch was to German panzer leaders in Europe. Here, McClure congratulates a Chinese general after the liberation of Nanning in July 1945 (*National Archives*)

USAAF transport force, including ATC aircraft pulled from the 'Hump' as Chinese ports re-opened, was committed to flying Chinese Nationalist troops throughout the country to disarm Japanese forces, rescue Allied prisoners and keep cities from the grasp of the Soviet Army – now occupying Manchuria – or the Chinese Communists. The large-scale commitment of transport aircraft was a crucial element of US policy, which was attempting to prevent a Chinese Civil War by stabilising the Nationalist government.

Transport aircraft played a vital role in China post-war, as they linked up US forces in-country with the huge naval presence in the Pacific and Marine Corps units in northern China (supported by Marine Corps and Navy transport aircraft). However, as US peace efforts failed and the Chinese Civil War escalated, the US military commitment contracted, ending with the Marine Corps withdrawal from northern China in 1949. By then, C-47s had already helped win the first 'battle' of the Cold War, in the Berlin airlift.

This is how many wartime C-47s ended their frontline careers – cannibalised for spare parts, with this aircraft photographed at a base in China. A considerable number of US transports were turned over to the Chinese Nationalists, and many of these aircraft, along with abandoned airframes such as this one (which was eventually returned to airworthiness), ended up serving into the 1960s (*National Archives*)

CONCLUSION

Transport aircraft played a key part in the Allied victory against a determined enemy in the Pacific and CBI. In the vanguard of this effort literally from start to finish was the C-47/R4D, as there was no better aircraft available to perform this mission, especially in 1942-44. The use of C-46/R5C and C-54/R5D combinations – more advanced designs – were more significant in the Pacific and CBI than in other wartime theatres, especially in 1945. Yet although larger aircraft had obvi-

Improvisation such as this became commonplace with the C-47. Here, a USAAF aircraft shows how spare wings could be flown under the belly in order to repair a damaged C-47 stuck at a forward airstrip. Originally demonstrated by CNAC in 1941 (creating the famous 'DC-2^1/$_2$'), replacement wings were subsequently fitted in the field on a number of occasions in the CBI and New Guinea (*National Archives*)

In the end, the use of C-47 series aircraft in the Pacific and CBI all depended upon the numbers of airframes that could be produced. The goal of having 14 TCGs in the ETO for D-Day dominated C-47 allocation until mid 1944, but after that more aircraft became available for other theatres and lend-lease (*Author's Collection*)

ous advantages in range and capacity, the C-47's ruggedness, reliability, ability to sustain battle damage, ease of maintenance and repair, and adaptability – all qualities that often do not show up in paper comparisons – made it invaluable. The reliability of the C-47, and its ability to operate out of forward fields with a minimal logistical footprint, made it more useful than aircraft that could generate more tons-per-mile under optimal conditions.

Although the C-47's early-1930s airframe technology meant that it carried much weight in its structure that could otherwise have been devoted to cargo load, this strength was appreciated when overloaded aircraft were dropped into short, rough forward airstrips or returned from frontline airdrop missions perforated with bullets. The build quality of the aircraft is why many Douglas twins are still flying today when advanced aircraft intended to replace them have largely become extinct.

The pattern for transport operations was set by decisive victories in each theatre where previously the Allies had experienced only defeat. Successes in Buna, Guadalcanal and the 'Admin Box' showed that fighting modern war – with the advantages in technology and support that were the western Allies' great strengths – in otherwise impossible environments required air transport.

The 1942 New Guinea campaign demonstrated the potential of air re-supply to the forces in Burma, while Guadalcanal showed both the effective use of transport aircraft in amphibious operations and the need for a joint transport organisation for the Central Pacific. The 'Admin Box', and the subsequent re-supply of Imphal and Kohima meant that the need for logistics support could be provided by air, minimising vulnerable lines of communications. The New Guinea and Burma campaigns were made possible by air transport.

The 'Hump' airlift was one of the great strategic air power victories of the war. It was expensive and inefficient – sea transport always moves bulk better – but irreplaceable to the US strategy of keeping China in the war. Transport aircraft (predominantly C-47s) kept China supplied and allowed it to function as a base for US air power. The publicity given to ATC and the 'Hump' mission, overshadowing the USAAF's contribution in Burma, reflected Washington's (unrealistic) perceptions of China's strategic importance. That the airlift could not counter superior Japanese strength on the ground does not detract from the magnitude of the accomplishment.

The operational environment was hostile throughout the Pacific and CBI. The long over-water segments throughout the south and central Pacific, the storms of the Aleutians, the Owen Stanleys, the 'Hump', and the Burmese jungles, each, in wartime conditions, claimed men and aircraft. But by the end of the war, US military transport aircraft not only helped the Allies prevail, but also transformed the world by trail blazing intercontinental air links that post-war technology strengthened.

In a sight repeated countless times during World War 2, a C-47 has its engine changed in the open somewhere in the Pacific. In the early stages of the conflict, when C-47 units deployed by air and operated for months in advance of the arrival of their ground echelons, such work stands and specialised equipment were rare, forcing improvisation. C-47 reliability and maintainability proved more important than pure carrying capability throughout the conflict (*National Archives*)

While the amounts of cargo moved by air in the Pacific theatres was only a fraction of the larger bulk shipments that arrived by sea, the timeliness and directness of air delivery was irreplaceable. Airlift kept US air power at Henderson Field in 1942 when even US Navy destroyers laden down with supplies could not get through. While tons of munitions delivered to remote docksides were often primarily a logistics problem, a smaller amount dropped into the hands of frontline fighting men that needed it on a just-in-time basis enabled Allied victories, and prevented the logistic 'tail' from devouring the combat 'teeth' in New Guinea, the Philippines, Burma and island battles such as Iwo Jima and Okinawa.

While USAAF troop carrier units and their Marine Corps counterparts deployed with a primary mission of performing parachute assaults, only a handful of these missions actually took place. Indeed, they were limited in scale and peripheral in mission compared to those in Europe. Rather, these units found themselves fully committed to transport missions.

The USAAF lacked pre-war experience in, or doctrine for, casualty evacuation, but soon developed great proficiency. Air casualty evacuation

A flightcrew from NATS unit VR-11 pose in front of their R4D-5 with some of the locally recruited cargo-handling personnel at Funafuti, on Ellis Island, in February 1945. In more remote areas, the culture shock of dealing for the first time with large numbers of outsiders who did not have to grow or hunt their own food, but rather had it arrive by aeroplane, led to the emergence of 'cargo cults' in the decades following the war. Some of these groups made models of what were obviously C-47s/R4Ds that served as the subject of veneration (*National Archives*)

both saved lives and demonstrated the commitment to fighting men and civilian voters alike that everything possible would be done to save lives.

The Marine Corps was able to draw on its unique pre-war air transport experience, allowing its R4Ds to sustain ground and air combat operations in amphibious campaigns throughout the Pacific. The US Navy continued its focus on transports as enabling forward-based fleet and air operations – the air counterpart of the massive fleet train that enabled sustained naval operations to an extent never seen before. Therefore, the two sea services used their R4Ds in different, but overlapping, roles.

'Back Stateside' – Capt Frank Libuse (holding the Papuan spear), Capt Gene Glotzbech, MSgt J W Gibbons (crew chief) and TSgt William Boffa (radio operator) got to take 41-7732 – the senior surviving C-47 in the SWPA, having arrived in-theatre in February 1942 – home to sell War Bonds in August 1944. The aircraft did a tour of plants building C-47s in an effort to show the workers the results of their labours. Glotzbech was one of the 33rd TCS pilots diverted to the New Caledonia-Guadalcanal airlift in October-November 1942 for a month of intensive combat operations, prior to flying on to New Guinea (*National Archives*)

Most of the support of the 'sharp end' was carried out by USAAF troop carrier and combat cargo squadrons (and their Marine Corps counterparts). Unlike similar units in other theatres, they rarely operated together within their controlling group. Units typically found themselves at the end of logistical shoestrings, with little help but their own resources, yet time after time they responded magnificently to the task at hand.

The division between the numbered air forces and ATC was artificial, and at times dangerously counterproductive. But given their different origins, the priority of the 'Hump' mission once it was given to ATC, and the need to keep open air routes in a global war in which theatre commanders rarely agreed on priorities and direction, it was probably the best solution to a command problem that still endures to this day.

The importance of organisations enabling joint and inter-Allied cooperation also enabled effective C-47 use. For example, transport aircraft proved vital to Allied special operations capability, providing airdrops and insertion and extraction of personnel in the Philippines, Burma and China. And although no one nation or service carried out these many tasks alone, they did, however, share a reliance on Douglas twins. Telling this story of US C-47 and R4D units sadly ignores the RAF, RAAF, RCAF and RNZAF Dakotas, CNAC DC-3s or US airliners that were also an integral part of ultimate victory in-theatre.

Sixty years after these events, C-47s still fly for a few air arms, whilst others earn a living as DC-3s. More still remain in museums. The 'Gooney Bird' is not yet an endangered species, but what has gone away is the world in which it was designed and, hastily, sent to war. The aeroplane itself was never intended to go to war, but when it did, it not only beat the enemy but transformed the world.

Those that built, flew and maintained the Douglas aircraft are now also fading from the scene, and with them goes the sights and sounds of what was done, even though a handful of their aeroplanes still survive. All that the future will know of them is what they have already recorded once they have, like the long-ago hypoxic crew singing while lost among the peaks, finally vanished into silence.

Also home from New Guinea, flight nurse 1Lt Frances Armin was part of 41-7732's 'back end' crew during its stateside trip. A veteran with more than 400 hours of 'green ink' combat flying in her logbook, Armin had performed many medical evacuation missions from New Guinea. When touring the Douglas plants, she would tell the 'Rosie the Riveters' in the audience of the flights their work had made possible (*National Archives*)

APPENDICES

C-47/R4D UNITS IN THE PACIFIC/CBI THEATRES OF OPERATION FROM DECEMBER 1941 TO 1946

Pacific Wing

Formed: 1/42 as Pacific Sector (HQ Hamilton, California), re-designated South Pacific Wing 7/42. Becomes Pacific Division (1943) (HQ Hickam HI), with subordinates West Coast Wing, South West Pacific Wing, Central Pacific Wing. Subordinated to ATC HQ, Washington, DC

North Pacific Area

Formed: 5/42. Subordinated to Pacific Ocean Areas

Alaska Wing
Formed: 10/42 (becomes Alaska Division in 1943), with HQ Edmonton, Alberta. Subordinated to ATC HQ, Washington, DC

Eleventh Air Force
Formed: 2/42 from Alaskan Air Force. Components include Eleventh AFSC(P) (6-8/42), Eleventh AFSC (8/42-46)

TCG (Provisional)
Formed: 7/43 Alaska

Subordinated to: Eleventh AF (7/43-3/44). Components 42nd TCS, 54th TCS (7/43-3/44)
Base: Elmendorf AK (7/43-3/44). Disbanded 3/44, HQ transferred to ATC

Squadrons – North Pacific

42nd TCS
Formed: 5/42 Alaska
Subordinated to: Eleventh AF (5-6/42), Eleventh AFSC (P) (6-8/42), Eleventh AFSC (8/42-7/43), TCG (P) (7/43-2/44)
Bases: Elmendorf AK (5/42-2/44), Lawson, GA (3-4/44). Training 2-4/44. Disbanded 4/44

54th TCS
Formed: 6/42 Hamilton, California
Subordinated to: 64th TCG (6/42), 315th TCG (6-10/42), Fourth AF (10-11/42), Eleventh AFSC (11/42-7/43), TCG(P) (7/43-2/44), Eleventh AF (2/44-48)
Bases: Bowman KY (6-8/42), Florence SC (8-10/42). Elmendorf AK (11/42-48). Used C-60s, re-equipped with C-47s 10/42. Used 1 C-47C, other transports as well

Central Pacific Area (direct command by Pacific Ocean Area) and Central Pacific Wing

Formed: 1942 (Hickam HI). Subordinate to Pacific Division ATC. HQ moves to Guam 1/45

Seventh Air Force (redesignated from Hawaiian AF 4/42)
Subordinated to Central Pacific Area (4/42-7/45), FEAF (14/7/45-end of war)

Eighth Air Force
HQ moves to Okinawa. (7/45-end of war)

Central Pacific Combat Air Transport Service,

Troop Carrier Group and Transport Aircraft Group
Formed: early 1943 Hawaii/Samoa as CENCATS. Elements re-designated TAG 3/43 (CENCATS remained operational). TCG Mar-Gils formed from TAG 11/44 to operate in Marshalls-Gilberts area. Disbanded 3/45 and routes taken over by NATS. Joint commands with USAAF, USMC and USN transports

419th TCG
Formed: 1/45 Guam. No organic aircraft. Operated detachments on Guam, Saipan, Tinian, Anguar and Iwo Jima. Disbanded Guam 2/46

Squadrons – Central Pacific

9th TCS
Formed: 12/40
Subordinated to: 63rd TCG (1/40-2/44), Seventh AF (2/44-7/45), VI Air Service Area Command (7-12/45), AAF Middle Pacific (12/45-1/46), Pacific Air Command (1/46), FEAF ASC (1/46), 54th TCW (1-2/46), 374th TCG (2-5/46), 54th TCW (5-10/46). Disbanded 10/46
Bases: Patterson OH (12/40-9/41), Brookley AL (9/41-5/42), William WI (5-9/42), Dodd TX (9-11/42), Stuttgart AR (11-12/42), Victorville CA (12/42-3/43), Sumner NM (3-5/43), Lawson GA (5-6/43), Grenada MS (6/43-1/44), Hickam HI (2/44-3/44), Abemama (3-8/44), Saipan (8/44-7/46), Guam (7-10/46). Received C-47/53s 9/42 (previously used C-33/39/50s). Some C-46s 6/44-46. Re-equipped with C-54s 1946

19th TCS
Formed: Hawaii 1/41
Subordinated to: Seventh AF (1/41-8/44) (operationally under TAG from 3/43), VI Air Service Area Command (8-12/45)
Bases: Hickam HI (1/41-5/42), John Rodgers HI (5/42-46). Formed with C-33s. 1942 receives impressed DC-3s, then C-53s, C-47s, C-45/46s and LB-30s/C-87s. Midway re-supply 1942. Flew missions to south/central Pacific.

311th TCS
Formed: 11/43
Subordinated to: 349th TCG (11/43-1/44), 1 TCC (12/44-2/45), VI Air Service Area Command (2-7/45), Seventh AF (7/45), AAF Middle Pacific (7/45-9/45), Eighth AFSC (10/45-2/46), 54th TCW (2-5/46)
Bases: Sedalia MO (11/43-1/44), Alliance NB (1-3/44), Baer IN (1/45), Kahoka HI (2/45), Bellows HI (2-7/45), Okinawa (8/45-5/46). Disbands 5/46. Formed with C-47s. Re-equips and deploys with C-46s to Hawaii 2/45

316th TCS
Formed: 12/43
Subordinated to: 61st TCW (12/43-2/44), 1st TCG (P) (2-7/44), VI Air Service Area Command (11/44-7/45), Seventh AF (7-9/45), Eighth AFSC (1/45-2/46), 54th TCW (2-3/46). Disbanded 3/46
Bases: Sedalia MO (12/43-1/44), Alliance BN (1-3/44), Mackall NC (3-9/44), Kahuku HI (11/44-2/45), Bellows HI (2-8/45), Okinawa (8/45-3/46).

Note
All HI-based USAAF, USMC and USN squadrons had aircraft forward in south (42-44) and central Pacific (44-46)

South Pacific Area (subordinated to Pacific Ocean Areas) and Southwest Pacific Area

ATC Southwest Pacific Wing

Formed: 4/44. Took over routes to the Philippines from Australia, New Guinea and the Solomons with formation of FEAF.

Far East Air Forces (Provisional)

Formed: 5/44
Subordinated to: SWPA GHQ
Components: Fifth and Thirteenth AFs (5/44-on), Seventh AF (7/45-on)

South Pacific Area Army Air Forces

Formed: Suva, Fiji
Subordinate to: SOPAC
Location: Noumea, New Caledonia (7/42), Espiritu Santo. Becomes Thirteenth AF 13/1/43

Fifth Air Force

Formed: Brisbane, Australia, 3/9/42 from Southwest Pacific Area Army Air Forces (formed 1/42), incorporating original Philippines-based Far East Air Force
Subordinated to: SWPA (9/42-3/44), FEAF(P) (3/44-46)

Thirteenth Air Force

Formed: Espiritu Santo 13/1/43 from South Pacific Area Army Air Forces
Subordinate to: SOPAC (1/43-3/44), FEAF(P) (5/44-46)

South Pacific Combat Air Transport Service

Formed: 11/42
Subordinate to: SOPAC. Joint USAAF-USMC operation (roughly 1-2 ratio). Disbanded 1/45. Subordinates include MAG-25 (42-45), 13th TCS (42-43), 33rd TCS (det.) (10-11/42), other USAAF assets attached throughout its operations

Directorate of Air Transport

Joint USAAF/RAAF/Australian civil/Netherlands military-civil air transport organisation
Formed: Australia 1/42

Components: 21 & 22 TCS (1-11/42), 6th TCS (10-11/42), 374th TCG (11/42-1/43), 317th TCG (1/43-3/43). Other US TCSs on temporary attachment. Disbanded 10/44. US components become 5298th TCW

54th TCW

Formed: 2/43 Brisbane, Australia
Subordinated to: Fifth AF (13/3/43-31/5/46)
Bases: Brisbane (2-5/43), Port Moresby (5/43-4/44) Nadzab (18/4/44-10/44), Biak (5/10/44-2/45), Leyte (14/3/45-6/45), Clark Field (6/45-9/45), Tachikawa, Japan (9/45-1/46), Manila (1-5/46)

322nd TCW

Formed: from 5298th TCW Hollandia 12/44
Subordinated to: FEAF (to end of war)
Components: 374th TCG
Bases: Hollandia (12/44-7/45), Manila (7/45-2/46). Disbanded

5298th TCW(P)

Formed: Australia 10/44 from US elements of DAT. Subordinated to FEAF(P). Redesignated 322nd TCW 12/44
Components: 22nd TCS (10-12/44), 33rd TCS (10-12/44), 8th CCS (11-12/44)
Bases: Brisbane (10-11/44), Port Moresby (11/44), Hollandia (12/44)

First Air Task Force

Formed as temporary HQ, Port Moresby. Subordinated to Fifth Air Force. Controlled four TCS mid-43

Second Air Task Force

Formed as temporary HQ, Nadzab. Subordinated to Fifth Air Force. Controlled several TCS autumn 1943-early 1944.

Group Level Units – SOPAC and SWPA

3rd ACG

Formed: 5/44 Drew CA
Subordinated: to Fifth AF on deployment
Bases: Lakeland FL (5-8/44), Alachua FL (8-10/44), Drew FL (10/44), Leyte (12/44-1/45), Mangaldan, Luzon (1-4/45), Laoag, Luzon (4-8/45), Ie Shima (8-10/45), Chitose, Japan (10/45-3/46). Intended to be spearhead of proposed air invasion of Mindanao with Chindit-type operations but instead integrated into FEAF

2nd CCG

Formed: 4/44 with C-47s
Subordinated to: 54th TCW (11/44-45)
Bases: Syracuse NY (5-10/44), Baer IN (10/44), Biak, New Guinea (11/44-5/45), Leyte (5/45-8/45), Okinawa (8-9/45), Yokota, Japan (9/45-1/46) then disbanded. Deployed 10/44 equipped with C-46s, received some C-47s

317th TCG

Formed: 2/42
Subordinated to: Fifth AF (1/43), DAT (1-3/43), 54th TCW (3/43-5/46)
Bases: Duncan TX (2/42-9/42), Bowman KY (9-10/42), Maxton NC (11-12/42), Garbutt, Australia (1/43). Deployed from US 1/43 with 52 C-47s. Port Moresby, New Guinea (1-2/43), Garbutt, Australia (exchanged aircraft with 374th TCG) (3-9/43), re-equipped with new C-47s (9/43), New Guinea (9/43-11/44), Philippines (11/44-5/48). Received some C-46s in 1944. Partially re-equipped with C-46s 9/45. Re-equipped with C-54s 1947

374th TCG

Formed: Australia 11/42 to command four already-deployed TCS (6th, 21st, 22nd, 33rd)
Subordinated to: DAT (11/42-3/43, 5/43-9/44), Fifth AF (3-5/43), 54th TCW (10/44), 5298th TCW(P) (10-12/44), 322nd TCW (12/44-5/46)
Bases: Brisbane, Australia (11-12/42), Port Moresby, New Guinea (12/42-10/43), Garbutt-Townsville, Australia (10/43-9/44), Nadzab, New Guinea (9/44-10/44), Biak, New Guinea (10/44-5/45), Nielson, Luzon (5/45-5/46). Partially re-equipped with C-46s 9/45. Disbanded 5/46. Half of 33rd TCS was detained in New Caledonia 10-11/42 and committed to Guadalcanal airlift before flying on to Australia. Used old transports (including DC-2/3/5, C-39, C-50/53s) and a few replacement C-47s until it became C-47-equipped through exchange of aircraft with 317th TCG 3/43

375th TCG

Formed: 11/42
Subordinated to: 54th TCW (7/43-46)
Bases: Bowman KY (11/42-1/43), Sedalia MO (1-5/43), Lautinburg NC (5-6/43), Baer IN (6/43), Brisbane, Australia (7/43), Port Moresby, New Guinea (7-8/43), Dobodura, New Guinea (8-12/43), Port Moresby, New Guinea (12/43-4/44), Nadzab, New Guinea (4-9/44), Sorido Biak, New Guinea (9/44-2/45), San Jose, Mindoro (2-5/45), Porac Luzon (5-8/45), Okinawa (8-9/45), Tachikawa, Japan (9/45-3/46) then disbanded. Equipped with C-47s, but also at least one B-17 per TCS as transports. Partially re-equipped with C-46s in 1944-45 (received first in 12/44)

403rd TCG

Formed: 12/42

Subordinated to: SCAT/Thirteenth AF (7/43-9/45). Moved to SPA 7-9/43, acquiring 13th TCS, transferring 63rd, 65th and 66th TCSs to first 54th TCW, then 433rd TCG. Disbanded 10/46

Bases: Bowman KY (12/42), Alliance NB (12/42-5/43), Pope NC (5-6/43), Baer IN (6-7/44), Espiritu Santo (7-8/44), Los Negros (8-10/44), Biak (10/44-6/45), Leyte (6/45-1/46), Clark (1-6/46), Manila (6-10/46). Only Thirteenth AF TCG. After formation of FEAF, centrally tasked by that HQ alongside Fifth AF units. Aircraft detached to SCAT operational control

433rd TCG

Formed: 2/43

Subordinated to: Fifth AF (8-9/43), 54th TCW (10/43-1/46)

Bases: Florence SC (2-8/43), Baer IN (8/43), moved to Pacific 8-11/43. Port Moresby, New Guinea (8/43-10/44), Biak, New Guinea (10/44-1/45), Tanauan, Leyte (1-5/45), Clark, Luzon (5-9/45), Tachikawa, Japan (9/45-1/46) then disbanded. C-47 equipped, but with a few B-17 transports. Flew C-46s starting in late 1944. Trained in glider–towing pre-deployment

Squadrons – SOPAC and SWPA

5th CCS

Formed: 5/44

Subordinated to: 2nd CCG (5/44-1/46)

Bases: Syracuse NY 5-10/44, Baer IN (10/44), Biak (11/44-5/45), Dulag, Leyte (5-8/45), Okinawa (8-9/45), Yokota, Japan (9/45-1/46). Formed with C-47s. Deployed with C-46s

6th CCS

Formed: 5/44

Subordinated to: 2nd CCG (5/44-1/46)

Bases: Syracuse NY (5-10/44), Baer IN (10/44), Biak (11/44-3/45), Samar (3/45), Dulag, Leyte (3-8/45), Okinawa (8-9/45), Yokota, Japan (9/45-1/46). Formed with C-47s. Deployed with C-46s

7th CCS

Formed: 5/44

Subordinated to: 2nd CCG (5-1/46)

Bases: Syracuse NY 5-10/44, Baer IN (10/44), Biak, New Guinea (11/44-3/45), Dulag, Leyte (3-8/45), Okinawa (8-9/45), Yokota, Japan (9/45-1/46). Formed with C-47s. Deployed with C-46s

8th CCS

Formed: 5/44

Subordinated to: 2nd CCG (5-11/44), 5298th TCW(P) (11-12/44), 2nd CCG (12/44-1/46)

Bases: Syracuse NY (5-10/44), Baer IN (10/44), Finschhafen, New Guinea (11/44-1/45), Biak, New Guinea (1/45-3/45), Dulag, Leyte (3-8/45), Okinawa (8-9/45), Yokota, Japan (9/45-1/46). Deployed with C-46s, used some C-47s in 1945

6th TCS

Formed: Olmstead PA 10/39

Subordinated to: 61st TCG (5/41-3/42), 315th TCG (3-6/42), 63rd TCG (6-9/42), Fifth AF (10/42-12/42), 374th TCG (12/42-5/46)

Bases: Williams WI (12/41-3/42), Dodd TX (9/42), Ward Field, Port Moresby, New Guinea (10/43), Garbutt Field, Australia (10/43), Nadzab, New Guinea (8-10/44), Biak, New Guinea (10/44-3/45), Tacloban, Leyte (3/45-1/46), Nielson, Luzon (1-5/46). Formed with six C-33/39s, received six C-53s 11/41, re-equipped with 13 C-47s 9/42. First to deploy to SWPA equipped with C-47s, arrived Australia 10/42

13th TCS

Formed: 12/40

Subordinated to: 61st TCG (12/40-10/42), USAAF SPA/Thirteenth AF (10-12/42), SCAT (12/42-7/44) (administratively under Thirteenth AF to 7/43), Thirteenth AF Service Command (7-9/43), 403rd TCG (9/43-10/46)

Bases: Patterson OH (12/40-7/41), Drew FL (7/41-5/42), Pope NC (5-8/42), Lockbourne OH (8-9/42), Plaines des Gaiacs, New Caledonia (10-12/42), Tontouta, New Caledonia (12/42-11/43), Espiritu Santo (11/43-8/44), Los Negros (8-9/44), Biak, New Guinea (9/44), Wakde, New Guinea (10/44), Biak, New Guinea (10/44-7/45), Dulag, Leyte (7/45-1/46), Clark, Luzon (1-6/46), Nichols, Luzon (6-10/46)

21st TCS

Formed: 4/42 in Australia

Subordinated: DAT (2/42-11/42), 374th TCG (11/42-1/46)

Bases: Essenden, Australia (3-10/42), Garbutt, Australia (10/42-1/43), Port Moresby, New Guinea (1/43-10/43), Garbutt, Australia (10/43-8/44), Finschhafen, New Guinea (8/44-8/45), Nielson, Luzon (8/45-1/46). Formed with B-18s, DC-2/3 (ex-KNILM/KLM), C-39, C-49s, C-53s, C-60s, B-17Cs, LB-30s. First C-47s arrived 4/42. Re-equipped with C-47s 3/43. Re-equipped with C-46s 6-7/1945

22nd TCS

(Subordination/aircraft same as 21st TCS)

Bases: Archerfield, Australia (2/42-2/43), Jackson Field, Port Moresby, New Guinea (2/43-10/43), Archerfield, Australia (10/43-8/44), Nadzab, New Guinea (8/44-10/44), Biak, New Guinea (10/44-8/45), Atsugi, Japan (9-12/45), Manila (12/45-1/46)

33rd TCS

Formed: 2/42

Subordinated to: 315th TCG (2/42-9/42), 374th TCG (11/42-2/46)

Bases: Olmstead PA (2-4/42), Florence SC (8-9/42), Det To New Caledonia (missions to Guadalcanal) (10-11/42), Cairns, Australia (11-12/42), Brisbane, Australia (12/42), Ward Field, Port Moresby, New Guinea (12/42-10/43), Townsville, Australia (10/43-4/44), Port Moresby, New Guinea (4/44-10/44), Hollandia, New Guinea (10/44-4/45), Nielson, Luzon (4/45-2/46), then disbanded. Received first aeroplane (C-53) 6/42, re-equipped with C-47s (deployed with 13), re-equipped with C-46s 1945. 10-11/42 six C-47s en route to Australia, det to New Caledonia

39th TCS

Formed: 2/42

Subordinated to: 317th TCG (2/42-8/49)

Bases: Duncan TX (2-6/42), Bowman KY (6-10/42), Lawson GA (10-12/42), Maxton NC (12/42), Garbutt, Australia (1-10/43), Port Moresby, New Guinea (10/43-4/44), Finschhafen, New Guinea (4/44), Cyclops, Hollandia, New Guinea (4-11/44), Leyte (11/44-3/45), Clark, Luzon (3-8/45), Kadena, Okinawa (8/45-10/46). Originally equipped with 13 C-47s, took over older aircraft in Australia. Re-equipped with C-47s in 1943 and C-46s in 1946

40th TCS

Formed: 2/42

Subordinated to: 317th TCG (2/42-8/49)

Bases: Duncan TX (2-6/42), Bowman KY (6-10/42), Lawson GA (10-12/42), Maxton NC (12/42), Garbutt, Australia (1-10/43), Port Moresby, New Guinea (10/43-4/44), Finschhafen, New Guinea (4/44), Hollandia, New Guinea (4-11/44), Leyte (11/44-3/45), Clark, Luzon (3-8/45), Kadena, Okinawa (8-10/45), Osaka, Japan (10/45-1/46), Tachikawa, Japan (1-10/46). Originally equipped with C-47s, took over older aircraft in Australia. Re-equipped with C-47s in 1943 and C-46s in 1945-46

41st TCS

Formed: 2/42

Subordinated to: 317th TCG (2/42-8/49)

Bases: Duncan TX (2-6/42), Bowman KY (6-10/42), Lawson GA (10-12/42),

Maxton NC (12/42), Garbutt, Australia (1-10/43), Port Moresby, New Guinea (10/43-4/44), Finschhafen, New Guinea (4/44), Cyclops, Hollandia, New Guinea (4-11/44), Leyte (11/44-3/45), Clark, Luzon (3-8/45), Kadena, Okinawa (8-10/45), Kimpo, Korea (10/45-1/46), Seoul, Korea (1-6/46). Equipped with new C-47s originally. Took over older aircraft on arrival in Australia. Re-equipped with C-47s in 1943 and with C-46s in 1946

46th TCS

Formed: 2/42

Subordinated to: 317th TCG (2/42-8/49)

Based: Duncan TX (2-6/42), Bowman KY (6-10/42), Lawson GA (10-12/42), Maxton NC (12/42), Garbutt, Australia (1-10/43), Port Moresby, New Guinea (10/43-4/44), Finschhafen, New Guinea (4-7/44), Hollandia, New Guinea (7-11/44), Leyte (11/44-3/45), Clark, Luzon (3-8/45), Kadena, Okinawa (8-10/45), Seoul, Korea (10/45-1/46), Tachikawa, Japan (1-6/46). Equipped with new C-47s originally. Took over older aircraft on arrival in Australia. Re-equipped with C-47s in 1943 and with C-46s in 1946

55th TCS

Formed: 11/42

Subordinated to: 375th TCG (11/42-3/46)

Bases: Bowman KY (11/42-1/43), Sedalia MO (1/43-5/43), Lautinburg-Maxton NC (5-6/43), Baer IN (6/43), Port Moresby, New Guinea (7-8/43), Dobodura, New Guinea (8-12/43), Port Moresby, New Guinea (1243-4/44), Nadzab, New Guinea (4-10/44), Biak, New Guinea (10/44-2/45), San Marcellino, Luzon (2-5/45), Porac, Luzon (6-8/45), Kadena, Okinawa (8-9/45), Tachikawa, Japan (9/45-3/46) then disbanded. Used C-47s in 1942-44 (plus 1+ B-17 transports 1943-45). Re-equipped with C-46 in 1944-45 and C-47s 10/45

56th TCS

Formed: 11/42

Subordinated to: 375th TCG (11/42-3/46)

Bases: Bowman KY (11/42-1/43), Sedalia MO (1/43-5/43), Lautinburg-Maxton NC (5-6/43), Baer IN (6/43), Port Moresby New Guinea (7-8/43), Dobodura, New Guinea (8-12/43), Port Moresby, New Guinea (12/43-4/44), Nadzab, New Guinea (4-10/44), Biak, New Guinea (10/44-2/45), San Jose, Mindoro (2/45-5/45), Porac, Luzon (5-8/45), Kadena, Okinawa (8-9/45), Tachikawa, Japan (9/45-3/46) then disbanded. Used C-47s in 1942-45 (plus 1+ B-17 transports 1943-45). Re-equipped with C-46s in 1944-46

57th TCS

Formed: 11/42

Subordinated to: 375th TCG (11/42-3/46)

Bases: Bowman KY (11/42-1/43), Sedalia MO (1/43-5/43), Lautinburg-Maxton NC (5-6/43), Baer IN (6/43), Port Moresby, New Guinea (7-8/43), Dobodura, New Guinea (8-12/43), Port Moresby, New Guinea (12/43-4/44), Nadzab, New Guinea (4-9/44), Biak, New Guinea (9/44-2/45), San Jose, Mindoro (2/45-5/45), Porac, Luzon (5-8/45), Kadena, Okinawa (8-9/45), Tachikawa, Japan (9/45-3/46) then disbanded. Used C-47s 1942-45 (plus 1+ B-17 transports 1943-45). Re-equipped with C-46s in 1944-46

58th TCS

Formed: 11/42

Subordinated to: 375th TCG (11/42-3/46)

Based: Bowman KY (11/42-1/43), Sedalia MO (1/43-5/43), Lautinburg-Maxton NC (5-6/43), Baer IN (6/43), Port Moresby, New Guinea (7-8/43), Dobodura, New Guinea (8-12/43), Port Moresby, New Guinea (12/43-4/44), Nadzab, New Guinea (4-9/44), Biak, New Guinea (9/44-3/45), San Jose, Mindoro (3/45-5/45), Porac, Luzon (5-8/45), Kadena, Okinawa (8-9/45), Tachikawa, Japan (9/45-3/46) then disbanded. Used C-47s 1942-45 (plus 1+ B-17 transports 1943-45). Re-equipped with C-46s in 1944-46

63rd TCS

Formed: 12/42

Subordinated to: 403rd TCG (12/42-5/46)

Bases: Bowman KY (12/42), Alliance NB (12/42-5/43), Pope NC (5/43-6/43),

Baer IN (6-7/43), Tontouta, New Caledonia (8/43), Espiritu Santo (8/43-8/44), Los Negros (8-10/44), Biak, New Guinea (10/44), Wakde, New Guinea (10/44), Noemfoor, New Guinea (10/44-5/45), Dulag, Leyte (5/45-1/46). Converted to C-46s 7-9/45

64th TCS

Formed: 12/42

Subordinated to: 403rd TCG (12/42-5/46)

Bases: Bowman KY (12/42), Alliance NB (12/42-5/43), Pope NC (5-6/43), Baer IN (6-7/43), Tontouta, New Caledonia (8/43), Espiritu Santo (8-11/43), Guadalcanal (11/43-9/44), Biak, New Guinea (9/44-10/44), Wakde, New Guinea (10/44), Noemfoor, New Guinea (10/44-1/45), Biak, New Guinea (1-7/45), Dulag, Leyte (7/45-1/46), Clark, Luzon (1-5/46) then disbanded. Equipped with C-47s, re-equipped with C-46s mid-1945

65th TCS

Formed: 12/42

Subordinated to: 403rd TCG (12/42-9/43), 54th TCW (9/43-10/43), 433rd TCG (10/43-2/45), 403rd TCG (2/45-5/46)

Bases: Bowman KY (12/42), Alliance NB (12/42-5/43), Pope NC (5/43-6/43), Baer IN (6-7/43), Port Moresby, New Guinea (7-9/43), Tsili Tsili, New Guinea (9-10/43), Port Moresby, New Guinea (11/43-10/44), Biak, New Guinea (10/44-1/45), Hill, Mindoro (1-2/45), Morotai (2-7/45), Dulag, Leyte (7/45-1/46), Clark, Luzon (1-5/46) then disbanded. Equipped with C-47s, re-equipped with C-46s starting 6/45

66th TCS

Formed: 12/42

Subordinated to: 403rd TCG (12/42-7/43), Fifth AF (7-9/43), 54th TCW (9/43-11/43), 433rd TCG (11/43-2/45), 403rd TCG (2/45-5/46)

Bases: Bowman KY (12/42), Alliance NB (12/42-5/43), Pope NC (5/43-6/43), Baer IN (6-7/43), Port Moresby, New Guinea (7-9/43), Nadzab, New Guinea (9/43-5/44), Tadji, New Guinea (5-6/44), Nadzab, New Guinea (6-11/44), Biak, New Guinea (11/44-1/45), Hill, Mindoro (1-2/45), Dulag, Leyte (2/45), Morotai (2-8/45), Dulag, Leyte (8/45-5/46) then disbanded. Equipped with C-47s, received C-46s mid-1945

67th TCS

Formed: 2/43

Subordinated to: 433rd TCG (2/43-1/46)

Bases: Florence SC (2-3/43), Sedalia MO (3-6/43), Lautinburg-Maxton NC (6-8/43), Baer IN (8/43), Port Moresby, New Guinea (8-11/43), Nadzab, New Guinea (11/43-7/44), Hollandia, New Guinea (7-10/44), Biak, New Guinea (10/44-1/45), Tanauan, Leyte (1-6/45), Clark, Luzon (6-8/45), Iwo Jima (8-9/45), Ie Shima (9/45), Tachikawa, Japan (9/45-1/46), then disbanded. Formed and deployed with C-47s, re-equipped with C-46s 1944

68th TCS

Formed: 2/43

Subordinated to: 433rd TCG (2/43-1/46)

Bases: Florence SC (2-3/43), Sedalia MO (3-6/43), Lautinburg-Maxton NC (6-8/43), Baer IN (8/43), Port Moresby, New Guinea (9-12/43), Nadzab, New Guinea (1-10/44) (det to Tadji, New Guinea 5-6/44), Biak, New Guinea (11/44-2/45) (det to Nadzab, New Guinea 11/44-1/45), Tanauan, Leyte (2-6/45), Clark, Luzon (6-8/45), Iwo Jima (8/45), Ie Shima (9/45), Tachikawa, Japan (9/45-1/46), then disbanded. Formed and deployed with C-47s, re-equipped with C-46s in 1944

69th TCS

Formed: 2/43

Subordinated to: 433rd TCG (2/43-1/46)

Bases: Florence SC (2-3/43), Sedalia MO (3-6/43), Lautinburg-Maxton NC (6-8/43), Baer IN (8/43), Port Moresby, New Guinea (9/43-1/44), Nadzab, New Guinea (1/44-1/45), Biak, New Guinea (1/45), Tanauan, Leyte (1/45-6/45), Clark, Luzon (6-8/45), Iwo Jima (8-9/45), Ie Shima (9/45), Tachikawa, Japan (9/45-1/46) then disbanded. Formed and deployed with C-47s. Re-equipped with C-46s 1944

70th TCS

Formed: 2/43

Subordinated to: 433rd TCG (2/43-1/46)

Based: Florence SC (2-3/43), Sedalia MO (3-6/43), Lautinburg-Maxton NC (6-8/43), Baer IN (8/43), Townsville, Australia (9/43), Port Moresby, New Guinea (9-10/43), Nadzab, New Guinea (10/43-7/44), Hollandia, New Guinea (7-10/44), Biak, New Guinea (10/44-2/45), Dulag, Leyte (2-4/45), Tanauan, Leyte (4-6/45), Clark, Luzon (6/45-8/45), Iwo Jima (8/45), Ie Shima (9/45), Tachikawa, Japan (9/45-1/46), then disbanded. Formed and deployed with C-47s, re-equipped with C-46s in 1944

318th TCS

Formed: 5/44

Subordinated to: 3rd ACG (5/44-3/46) (administratively, operationally under 54th TCW or FEAF)

Based: Mackall NC (5-8/44), Donnellon FL (8-9/44), Mackall NC (9/44), Baer IN (9-10/44), Nadzab, New Guinea (10/44-1/45), Leyte (1/45), Mangaldan, Luzon (1-4/45), Laoag, Luzon (4-8/45), Ie Shima (8-9/45), Atsugi, Japan (9-10/45), Chitose, Japan (10/45-3/46) then disbanded

2nd ERS

Subordinated to: Fifth AF (7/44-6/45), Thirteenth AF (6-9/45). Operated in small detachments. Had a few C-47s among other types

3rd ERS

Subordinated to: Fifth AF (6-9/45). Operated in small detachments in the Philippines. Used a few C-47s along with other types

6th ERS

Subordinated to: Fifth AF. Operated from Ie Shima and Okinawa 7-9/45. Some C-47s

Combat Replacement Training Center

Nadzab (44-45). Used C-47s to train incoming replacement crews

US Navy and Marine Corps

US Navy and Marine Corps transport and utility squadrons were primarily administrative rather than tactical headquarters. Headquarters were in an area suitable for base maintenance, and R4Ds would be detached for service in forward areas, singly or in groups, for substantial periods. NATS units were considerably larger than Marine Corps or USAAF squadrons.

Naval Air Transport Service

Pacific Wing formed 10/42 and reorganised subordinate to Command, Air Transport Squadrons, West Coast 2/43. West Coast Wing formed 3/43 and subordinate to Command, Air Transport Squadrons, West Coast (formed 2/43) and disbanded 3/45. Asiatic Wing formed 8/45

US Navy Squadrons – NATS

VR-2

Formed: Alameda CA 12/12/41. Responsible for all Pacific NATS operations. Forward HQ Pearl Harbor 9/42. Becomes all-flying-boat unit 3/43

VR-3

Formed: Olathe KS 12/12/41, originally for operations in US, later included flights to Pacific

VR-4

Formed: Oakland 3/43. Took over landplanes from VR-2. Responsible for Pacific NATS landplane operations.

VR-5

Formed: NAS Sand Point Seattle 24/6/43 from VR-2 to handle all services to and in Alaska

VR-6

Formed: NAS Miami 1943. Deployed to Samar with R4Ds, other types, 7/45

VR-11

Formed: Oakland 9/43. Moved to Honolulu 12/43. Became largest unit in US armed forces with 700-1000 aircrew. VJ-Day had ten R4Ds (plus 90 R5Ds)

VR-13

Formed: Oakland 6/44. Moved to Los Negros, Manus Island 4/45

Note
All landplane units used R4Ds with smaller numbers of R5D, R5C, RY, R5O Lodestar and other transports. Services in SOPAC and SWPA

VRE-1

Formed: from VR-11 in Honolulu 1944. Guam 1944. Main equipment R5Ds Intercontinental medical evacuation specialists

US Navy Squadrons - Others

VRF-3

Formed: 1943 NAS Terminal Island CA. Delivered R4Ds worldwide as part of Navy Ferry Command, which transferred to NATS as Ferry Wing (12/43)

VRJ-1

Based Hawaii. Included a few R4Ds, including VIP transports. Transferred to NATS in 1945

VH-2, 3, 5 and 6

Formed: 1944. R4Ds removed 12/44. Served in Pacific

VE-1

Formed: 12/44 from R4Ds from VH-1 and flying-boats from VH-2. Served in Pacific. Based Guam in 1944-45. Used for casualty evacuation

VE-2

Formed: 12/44 with R4Ds from VH-3/4. Served in Pacific. Based Guam 1944-45. Used for casualty evacuation

VE-3

Formed: 12/44 with R4Ds from VH-5/6. Served in Pacific. Used for casualty evacuation

Marine Corps Air Groups

MAG-15

Formed: 3/42

Subordinated to: TAG (4/44-10/44), ATG (10/44), TCG Mar-Gils (11/44-3/45), TAG (3/45-9/45)

Bases: San Diego (3/42-3/44) (training), Apamama (4/44), Kwajalein (4/44-3/45), Ewa HI (3/45-9/45)

MAG-21

Formed: Ewa HI 8/41

Bases: Deployed 2/43 to Russells (2/43-11/43), Efate (11/43-6/44), Orote, Guam (8/44-12/44), Agano, Guam (12/44-8/45)

MAG-25

Formed: 6/42

Subordinated to: SCAT (11/42-2/45)

Bases: San Diego (6-8/42), Ewa HI (8-9/42), New Caledonia (9/42-7/44), Bougainville (7/44-8/45), Okinawa (9/45), Tsingtao, China (10/45-1947)

Marine Corps Squadrons

VMJ/R-152

Formed: from VMJ-1 Quantico VA (7/41). Re-equipped with R4D mid-1942. Deployed 10/42

Subordinated to: MAG-15 (12/41-10/42), MAG-25 (10/42-10/45)

Bases: San Diego (12/41-10/42), New Caledonia (10/42-8/44), Redesignated 6/44. Bougainville (8/44-10/45) (missions in 1944-45 to Philippines and Okinawa)

VMJ/R-153

Formed: San Diego 3/41-2/43. Deployed 3/43 to New Caledonia

Subordinated to: MAG-25 (3/43-8/45)

Bases: Bougainville (6/44-10/45), Tsingtao, China (10/45-49). Partially re-equipped with R5Ds. Last Marine Corps air unit out of North China 1/49

VMJ/R-252

Formed: from VMJ-2 Ewa HI 7/41 with R3Ds. Midway re-supply

Subordinated to: MAG-21 (12/41-8/42), Hawaii commands (8/42-3/44), MAG-14 (4/44-4/45), MAG-21 (4/45)

Bases: Kwajalein (3/44), Marshalls (9/44), Guam (4/45). Re-equipped with R4Ds mid-1942. Re-equipped with R5Cs 1943 to mid-1944

VMJ/R-253

Formed: San Diego 2/42

Subordinated to: MAG-25 (9/42-6/44), TAG (8-10/44), MAG-21 (10/44-8/45)

Bases: Ewa HI (3/42), New Caledonia (9/42-8/44) (operating throughout Solomons), Apanama (8/44), Tarawa (9/44), Guam (10/44-8/45). Re-equipped with R5Cs 3/45

VMR-352

Formed: 4/43 Cherry Point NC

Subordinated to: MAG-15 (3-9/45)

Bases: John Rogers HI (mid-1944 to 1945), Guam (1945). Converted to R5C mid-1944

VMR-353

Formed: 3/43

Subordinated to: MAG-15. Re-equipped with R5Cs in 1944

VMR-952

Formed: 6/43

Subordinated to: TAG (1944-45). Used R5Cs

VMR-953

Formed: 2/44

Subordinated to: MAG-15 (3-9/45). Used R5Cs

AES-45

Formed: North Island CA 1943. Missions included ferrying USMC transports to Pacific

US Coast Guard

R4Ds used by SAR detachments at Port Angeles WA, San Francisco CA, other bases (1944 onwards)

India-China-Burma theatre *(divided into China and India-Burma Sectors 7/43, theatres 10/44-9/45)*

India-China Wing ATC

Formed: 12/42 from Indian Sector (formed 1/42). Becomes India-China Division 12/43

Subordinates: Assam Wing, India Wing, Bengal Wing, China Wing

1st FG

Formed: 3/42. Deployed to India 3/42 with 3rd, 6th, and 13th Ferrying Squadron (ATC)

Subordinated to: Tenth Air Force (4-12/42) as Assam Burma China Ferry Command. Incorporated in ICW 12/42

Bases: Pope NC (3/42), Charleston SC (3/42), Karachi (4-7/42), Dinjan (7-12/42). Disbanded as ATC reorganised (12/43). Equipped with C-47s (1+ ex-RAF) and C-48/50/53s.

22nd FG/TG (ATC)

Formed: 2/43. Redesignated 7/43

Subordinated to: ICW

Bases: Chabua, India (2-4/43), Jorhat, India (4/43-12/43). Disbanded 12/43

28th TG (ATC)

Formed: 6/43

Subordinated to: ICW

Based: Tezpur, India (6/43-12/43). Disbanded 12/43

29th TG (ATC)

Formed: 6/43

Subordinated to: ICW

Based: Sookerating, India (6/43-12/43). Disbanded 12/43

30th TG (ATC)

Formed: 6/43

Subordinated to: ICW

Based: Mohanbari, India (6/43-12/43). Disbanded 12/43

3rd FS

Subordinated to: 1st Ferrying Group (4-12/42)

Bases: Pope NC (3/42), Charleston SC (3/42) and Karachi (4-5/42), New Malir Cantt, Chabua (7-12/43), India. Disbanded as ATC reorganised

6th FS

Subordinated to: 1st Ferrying Group (4-12/42)

Bases: Pope NC (3/42), Charleston SC (3/42), Karachi, India (4-7/42), Chabua, India (7-12/43). Disbanded as ATC reorganised

13th FS

Subordinated to: 1st Ferrying Group (4-12/42)

Bases: Pope NC (3/42), Charleston SC (3/42), Karachi (4-5/42), Chabua, India (5-7/42), Sookerating, India (8-12/43). ICW(ATC) (12/42-12/43). Disbanded as ATC reorganised

77th FS/TS (ATC)

Formed: 2/43. Redesignated 7/43

Subordinated to: 22nd FG/TG

Bases: Chabua, India (2-4/43), Jorhat, India (4-12/43. Disbanded 12/43

78th FS/TS (ATC)
Formed: 2/43. Redesignated 7/43
Subordinated to: 22nd FG/TG
Bases: Chabua, India (2-4/43), Jorhat, India (4-10/43), Sookerating, India (10-12/43). Disbanded 12/43

88th FS/TS (ATC)
Formed: 5/43. Redesignated 7/43
Subordinated to: 22nd FG/TG, resubordinated to 28th TG late 1943
Bases: Ondals, India (5-6/43), Karachi, India (7-12/43). Disbanded 12/43

96th TS (ATC)
Formed: 6/43. Tezpur, India (6/43-12/43), Disbanded 12/43

97th TS (ATC)
Formed: 6/43
Subordinated to: 28th TG.
Based: Tezpur, India (6/43-12/43). Disbanded 12/43

98th TS (ATC)
Formed: 6/43
Subordinated to: 28th TG. Tezpur, India (6/43-12/43). Disbanded 12/43

99th TS (ATC)
Formed: 6/43
Subordinated to: 29th TG. Disbanded 12/43
Based: Sookerating, India (6-12/43)

100th TS (ATC)
Formed: 6/43
Subordinated to: 29th TG. Disbanded 12/43
Based: Sookerating, India (6-12/43)

301st TS (ATC)
Formed: 6/43
Based: Sookerating, India (6-12/43). Disbanded 12/43

302nd TS (ATC)
Formed: 6/43
Subordinated to: 30th TG
Based: Mohanbari, India (6-12/43). Disbanded 12/43

303rd TS (ATC)
Formed: 6/43
Subordinated to: 30th TG
Based: Mohanbari, India (6-12/43). Disbanded 12/43

304th TS (ATC)
Formed: 6/43
Subordinated to: 30th TG
Based: Mohanbari, India (6-12/43). Disbanded 12/43

CBI – Higher Headquarters

US Army Air Forces China
Formed: 7/45. Headquarters for Tenth and Fourteenth AFs

Tenth Air Force and Fourteenth Air Force
Formed: 3/43 from China Air Task Force (formed 7/42)

Eastern Air Command
Formed: 12/43. Joint RAF/USAAF. Disbanded 5/45

Third Tactical Air Force
Disbanded 11/44

Troop Carrier Command
Subordinated to: EAC (12/43-5/44), Third TAF (5-6/44). Given operational control over all transport units supporting forces in Burma (including forces in northern Burma). Disbanded 6/44

Combat Cargo Task Force
Joint USAAF/RAF/RCAF. Formed 15/9/44 to replace TCC. Inactivated 6/45

69th CW
Formed: China 9/43
Subordinated to: Fourteenth AF (9/43-8/45) and Tenth AF (8-12/45)
Bases: Kunming, China (9/43-1/45), Tsuyung, China (1-4/45), Kunming, China (4-12/45). Designated BW (9-12/43)

CBI – Group Level Units

1st ACG
Formed: India 3/44
Subordinated to: transport (later 319th TCS), plus fighter, bomber and liaison sections (later squadrons)
Bases: Hailakandi, India (3-5/44), Asansol, India (5/44-10/45)

2nd ACG
Formed: Drew FL 4/44
Subordinated to: 317th TCS, plus fighter, bomber, liaison squadrons
Bases: Drew FL (4-9/44), arrived India 9-11/44, Kalaikunda, India (11/44-10/45). Disbanded 11/45

1st CCG
Formed: Bowman KY 4/44. Arrived India 8/44
Subordinated to: CCTF (9/44-1945)
Bases: Sylhet, India (8-11/44), Tulihal, India (11-12/44), Tsuyung, China

(12/44-1/45), Dohazari, India (1-5/45), Hathazari, India (5-8/45). Re-equipped with C-46s 6/45. Redesignated 512th TCG 9/45

3rd CCG
Formed: India 6/44
Subordinated to: Third TAF (6-8/44), Tenth AF/CCTF (9/44-5/45), NBATF (5-6/45), ATC (6-9/45)
Bases: Sylhet, India (6-8/44), Dinjan, India (8/44-1/45), Myitkyina, Burma (6-9/45). Redesignated 513th TCG 9/45. Received C-46s in 1945

4th CCG
Formed: 6/44. Arrived India 11/44
Subordinated to: Tenth AF/CCTF (9/44)
Bases: Syracuse NY (6-8/44), Bowman (KY 8-11/44), Sylhet, India (11/44-12/44), Agartala, India (12/44-1/45), Chittagong, India (1-6/45), Namponmao, Burma (6-11/45), Pandaveswar, India (11/45-1/46), Panagarh,

85

India (1-2/46), then disbanded. Equipped with C-46s before deployment, re-acquiring some C-47s in CBI.

1st TCG(P)

Formed: 2/45

Subordinated to: CCTF. Palel, India. Included the 317th, 319th TC and 1st CCS (on detachment). 5/45 moved to northern Burma

64th TCG (Reinforced)

As Arrowhead Force, deployed from MTO 3/44. Arrived Gaya, India 4/44. 4th, 16th, 17th, 18th, 35th TCS. Returned to MTO 7/44

443rd TCG

Formed: 10/43. Training in US 10/43-2/44 (309th, 310th TCS). HQ only deployed to CBI 2/44, taking over four C-47 squadrons in-theatre

Subordinated to: Tenth AF (3/44-6/45), AAF I-B Theatre (6-12/45). Operationally under TCC (3-5/44), EAC (5-9/44), Combat Cargo Task Force (CCTF) (9/44-6/45), ATC (6/45-12/45). 1, 2, 27th (3-5/44), 315th TCS, 1st CCS (9/44 det). Re-equipped with C-46 in 1945. China (8/45). Disbanded 12/45

512th TCG

Formed: 9/45 from redesignation of 1st CCG. Liuchow, China (9-10/45), Kiangwan, China (10-12/45). Disbanded 12/45

513th TCG

Formed: 9/45 from redesignation of 3rd CCG

North Burma Air Task Force

Formed and operated May-August 1945 to support the deployment of Chinese forces from Burma. Multiple squadrons assigned on detachment

CBI – Squadrons

1st CCS

Formed: Bowman KS 4/44, arrived India 8/44

Subordinated to: 1st CCG (4/44-6/45) (det to 443rd TCG 9/44, det to 1st TCG(P) 5/45), Fourteenth AF (6-8/45)

Bases: Sylhet, India (8-11/43) (detachments to Yunnani, China 9-10/44 and Hathazari, India 10-11/44), Tulihal, India (11-12/44), Tsuyung, China (12/44-1/45), Hsinching, China (1-8/45) (detachment at Liangshan, China 3-7/45), Chunking, China (9/45). Redesignated 326th TCS 9/45. Received C-46s in 1945

2nd CCS

Formed: 4/44, arrived India 8/44

Subordinated to: 1st CCG (4-7/45), ATC (7-10/45)

Bases: Sylhet, India (8-11/44) (detachment to Yunnani, China 9/44), Imphal, India (12/44), Tsuyung, China (12/44-2/45), Dohazari, India (2-5/45), Hathazari, India (5-10/45). Redesignated 327th TCS 10/45. Received C-46s in 1945

3rd CCS

Formed: 4/44, Bowman KY. Arrived India 8/44

Subordinated to: 1st CCG (4/44-6/45), ATC (6-9/45)

Bases: Sylhet, India (8-10/44) (detachment to Yunnani, China 9-10/44), Tulihal, India (11/44-4/45), Hathazari, India (4-8/45), Luliang, China (8-9/45). Redesignated 328th TCS 9/45. Received C-46s in 1945

4th CCS

Formed: 4/44, Bowman KY. Arrived India 8/44.

Subordinated to: 1st CCG (4/44-9/45), 69th CW (9/45)

Based: Sylhet, India (9-11/44) (detachment to Yunnani, China 9-10/44), Tulihal, India (11-12/44), Chengkung, China (12/44-2/45), Dohazari, India (2/45-8/45), Liuchow, China (8-9/45). Redesignated 329th TCS 9/45. Received C-46s in 1945

9th CCS

Formed: 5/44

Subordinated to: 3rd CCG (5/44-10/45)

Bases: Sylhet, India (6/44-7/44), Moran, India (7-12/44), Warazup, Burma (12/44-1/45), Myitkyina, Burma (1/45-10/45). Formed with C-47s. Received C-46s in 1945. Redesignated 330th CCS 10/45

10th CCS

Formed: 6/44

Subordinated to: 3rd CCG (6-10/45)

Bases: Sylhet, India (6-8/44), Deragon, India (8/44), Dinjan, India (8/44-6/45), Myitkyina, Burma (6-10/45). Formed with C-47s. Received C-46s in 1946. Redesignated 331st TCS (10/45)

11th CCS

Formed: 6/44

Subordinated to: 3rd CCG (6/44), 443rd TCG (6-8/44), 3rd CCG (9/44-1/45), Tenth AF (1-4/45), Fourteenth AF (4-10/45)

Bases: Sylhet, India (6/44-4/45) (det to Sookerating, India 6-7/44), Yunnani, China (4-6/45), Luliang, China (6-10/45). Redesignated 332nd TCS (10/45)

12th CCS

Formed: 6/44

Subordinated to: 3rd CCG (6/44-10/45)

Bases: Sylhet, India (6/44), Fenny, India (6/44), Moran, India (7/44-1/45), Tulihal, India (4-5/45), Ledo, India (5-6/45), Myitkyina, Burma (6-10/45). Redesignated 333rd TCS (10/45). Formed with C-47s. Received some C-46s in 1945

13th CCS

Formed: 6/44

Subordinated to: 4th CCG (6/44-12/45)

Bases: Syracuse NY (6/44), Bowman KY (8-11/44), Sylhet, India (11/44-1/45), Argartala, India (1/45), Chittagong, Burma (1-6/45) (det. to Tulihal, India (4-6/45), Namponmao, Burma (6/45-11/45), Ondal, India (11-12/45). Formed with C-47s and re-equipped with C-46s in 1944. Disbanded 12/45

14th CCS

Formed: 6/44

Subordinated to: 4th CCG (6/44-12/45)

Bases: Syracuse NY (6/44), Bowman KY (8-11/44), Sylhet, India (11/44-1/45), Argartala, India (1/45), Chittagong, Burma (1-6/45), Namponmao, Burma (6/45-11/45), Ondal, India (11/44-2/46). Formed with C-47s, re-equipped with C-46s in 1944. C-47s also used for airdrops in Burma. Disbanded 2/46

15th CCS

Formed: 6/44

Subordinated to: 4th CCG (6/44-12/45)

Bases: Syracuse NY (6/44), Bowman KY (8-11/44), Sylhet, India (11-1/45), Argartala, India (1/45), Chittagong, Burma (1-6/45), Namponmao, Burma (6/45-11/45), Ondal, India (11-12/45). Formed with C-47s and used for airdrops in Burma. Re-equipped with C-46s in 1944. Disbanded 12/45

16th CCS

Formed: 6/44

Subordinated to: 4th CCG (6/44-9/45), Tenth AF (9-10/45), 4th CCG (10-12/45)

Bases: Syracuse NY (6-8/44), Bowman KY (8-11/44), Sylhet, India (11/44-12/44), Agartala, India (12/44-1/45), Chittagong, Burma (1-6/45), Namponmao, Burma (6-9/45), Ledo, Burma (9-10/45), Namponmao, Burma (10-11/45), Ondal, India (11-12/45), then disbanded. Formed with C-47s. Re-equipped with C-46s. Re-acquired some C-47s in-theatre

1st TCS

Formed: Fairfield Air Depot 1935. Arrived India 2/43
Subordinated to: Tenth AF (2/43), India-China Wing ATC (2-3/43), Tenth AF (3-12/43), TCC (12/43-3/44), 433rd TCS (3/44-12/45)
Bases: Chabaur, India (2-3/43), New Delhi, India (3-10/43) (several detachments in India and China), Sookerating, India (10/43-4/45), Warazup, Burma (4-6/45), Dinjan, India (6-8/45), Chihkiang, China (8-9/45), Hankow, China (9-11/45), Shanghai, China (11-12/45) then disbanded. Re-equipped with C-46s en masse 4/45

2nd TCS

Formed: 1935, Olmstead PA
Subordinated to: Tenth AF (2-3/43), ATC (3-7/43), Assam Air Base Command (7-12/43), TCC (12/43-3/44), 443rd TCG (3/44-12/45)
Bases: Stout IN (5-7/42), Kellogg MI (7-8/42), Bowman KY (8-10/42), Pope NC (10/42-1/43). Arrived India 2/43. Yangkai, China (2-7/43), Dinjan, India (7/43-8/44), Shingbwiyang, Burma (8/44-1/45), Dinjan, India (1/45-8/45), Chihkiang, China (8-9/45), Hankow, China (9-11/45). Disbanded 12/45. Received first C-46s in 4/45, re-equipped by 7/45

27th TCS

Formed: 2/42
Subordinated to: 89th TCG (2-6/42), 10th TCG (6/42-12/43), Tenth AF (1/44-3/44), 443rd TCG (3/44-5/44), 69th CW (5/44-7/45)
Bases: Daniel GA (2-3/42), Harding LA (3-6/42), Kellogg MI (6-8/42), Bowman KY (8-10/42), Pope NC (10/42), Lawson GA (12/42-2/43), Donnellon FL (2-12/43), Sylhet, India (1-5/44), Yunnani, China (5/44-2/45) (dets to Chanyi, Chengtun, Kunming, China), Chengkung, China (2-8/45), Liangshan, China (8-12/45). Equipped with C-48/49/53s as training unit., before eventually deploying with C-47s. Transferred to China to re-supply the Chinese advance on the Salween River. Re-equipped with C-46s mainly after VJ-Day

315th TCS

Formed: 1/44
Subordinated to: TCC (1-3/44), 443rd TCG (3/44-12/45)
Bases: Dinjan, India (1/44), Sylhet, India (1-6/44), Sookerating, India (6/44), Moran, India (6/44), Sookerating, India (7-8/44) (dets to Shingbwiyang, Burma (7-8/44) and Ledo, India (7-8/44)), Ledo, India (8/44-5/45), Dinjan, India (5-8/45), Chihkiang, China (9/45), Hankow, China (9-10/45), Shanghai, China (9-12/45), then disbanded. Formed with C-47s. Re-equipped with C-46s starting 5/45, concluding after VJ-Day

317th TCS(C)

Formed: 5/44
Subordinated to: 2nd ACG (5/44) and 1st TCG(P)
Bases: Mackall NC (5-6/44), Alachua FL (6/44), Donnellon FL (6-8/44), Mackall NC (8-9/44), Baer IN (8-9/44), Sylhet, India (11/44), det to Tuhhal, India (11/44), Bikram, India (11-12/44), Myitkyina, Burma (12/44-1/45), Kalaikunda, India (1-2/45), dets to Dinjan, India (1/45) and Kiram, India (1/45), Palel, India (2-4/45), Kalaikunda, India (4-6/45), dets to Akyab, Burma (4-5/45) and Comilla, India (5/45), Ledo, India (6-9/45), Liangshan, China (9-11/45), Kunming, China (11/45), Salua, India (11-12/45), Hijiki, India (12/45-1/46), Titagurh, India (1-2/46), then disbanded. Deployed with C-47s. Largely re-equipped with C-46s mainly after VJ-Day

319th TCS(C)

Formed: 9/44 from Transport Squadron/Section, 1st ACG
Subordinated to: (operational) CCTF (9/44-2/45), 1st TCG (P) (2-5/45), Tenth AF (5-9/45) (part of 1st ACG until 9/45, then 69th CW)
Bases: Asanol, India (9-12/44), forward bases in Burma (12/44-5/45), Warazup, Burma (5-9/45), Loping, China (9-10/45), Huhsien, China (10/45-11/45), India (11-12/45). Disbanded 12/45

322nd TCS

Formed: 9/44 from redesignation of Fourteenth AF Transport Section. Re-equipped with C-46s in 1945
Subordinated to: Fourteenth AF (9/44-8/45) and Tenth AF (8-9/45)

326th TCS

Formed: redesignated from 1st CCS 9/45
Subordinated to: 69th CW (9-11/45), Fourteenth AF (12/45)
Bases: Chunking, China (9-11/45), Piardoba, India (11-12/45). Disbanded 12/45

327th TCS

Formed: redesignated from 2nd CCS 10/45
Subordinated to: Fourteenth AF (10-12/45)
Based: Peishiyi, China (10-12/45). Disbanded 12/45

328th TCS

Formed: redesignated from 3rd CCS 9/45
Subordinated to: 69th CW (9-11/45)
Bases: Kunming, China (9-11/45), Kharagpur, India (11-12/45). Disbanded 12/45

329th TCS

Formed: redesignated from 4th CCS 9/45
Subordinated to: 1st CCS
Bases: Liuchow, China (9-10/45), Hankow, China (10-11/45). Disbanded 12/45

330th TCS

Formed: redesignated from 9th CCS 10/45
Subordinated to: 513th TCG
Based: Shanghai, China (10/45-4/46). Disbanded

331st TCS

Formed: redesignated from 10th CCS 10/45
Subordinated to: 513th TCG (10/45-1/46)
Based: Shanghai, China (10/45-1/46). Disbanded

332nd TCS

Formed: redesignated from 11th CCS 9/45
Subordinated to: 513th TCG (10/45-4/46), AAF China (4-6/46), US Army Forces China (6/46-4/47)
Bases: Shanghai, China (10/45-6/46), Peking, China (6/46-4/47). Disbanded

333rd TCS

Formed: redesignated from 12th CCS 9/45
Subordinated to: 513th TCG (10/45-1/46)
Based: Shanghai (10/45-1/46). Disbanded

Transport Section/Squadron (Commando)

Formed: redesignated 319th TCS (9/44)
Subordinated to: 1st ACG (3-9/44)
Bases: Hailakandi, India (3-5/44), Asansol, India (5/44-9/44) (operating from forward bases in Burma in support of Chindits)

Fourteenth AF Transport Section

Formed: 3/43 by redesignating CATF Transport Section, which became 322nd TCS 9/44
Subordinated to: Fourteenth AF (3/43-9/44), Chinese-American Composite Wing (4/44), 69th CW

CATF Transport Section

Formed: 1/42 (1 C-47)
Subordinated to: CATF (1/42-3/43)

7th ERS

Subordinated to: Tenth AF
Based: Agartala, India (1-6/45)

8th ERS

Subordinated to: Fourteenth AF
Bases: Operated in China in small detachments with C-47s and helicopters (5-9/45)

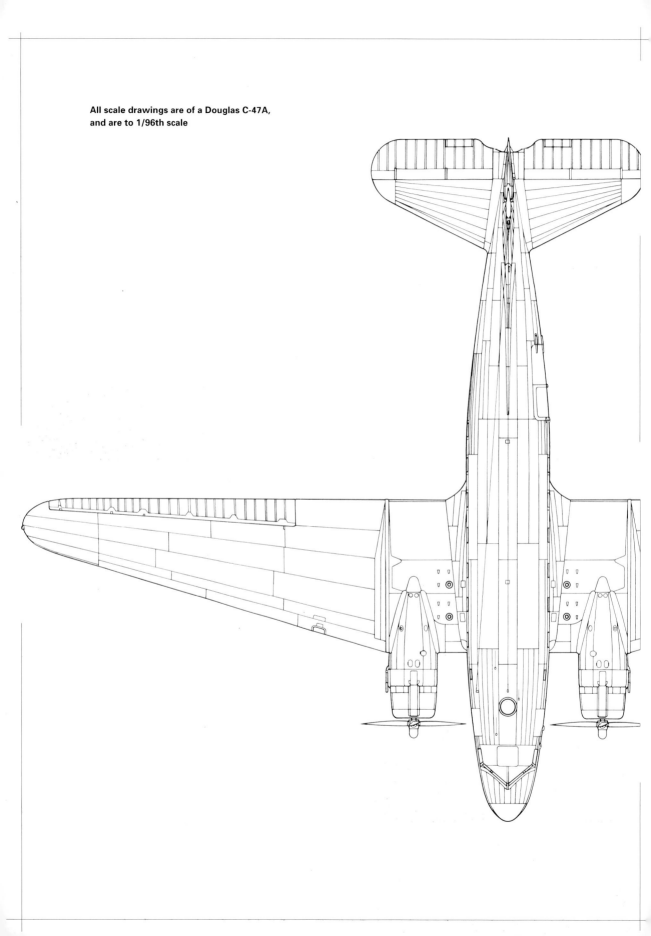

All scale drawings are of a Douglas C-47A,
and are to 1/96th scale

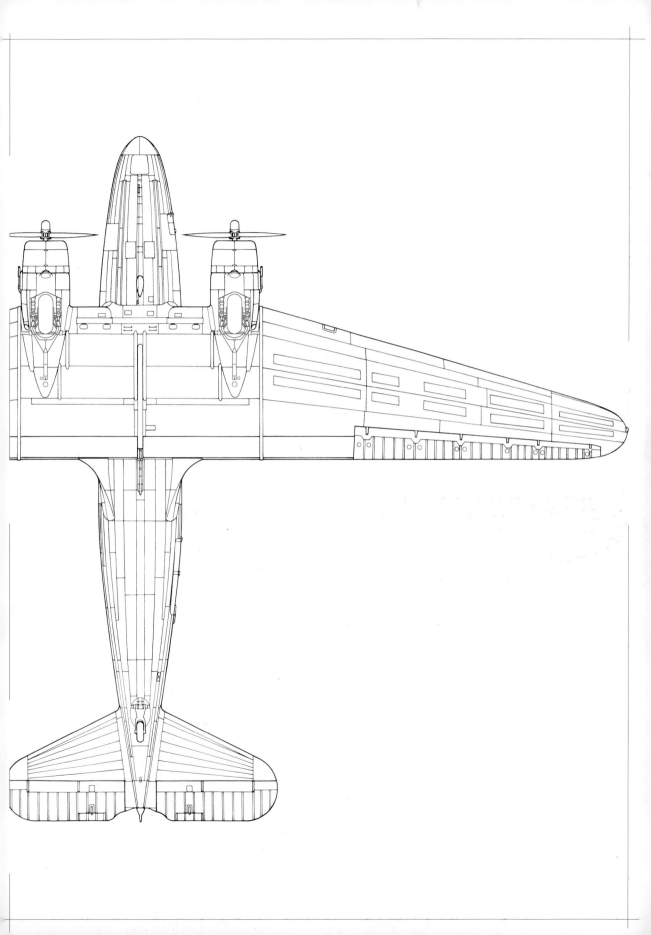

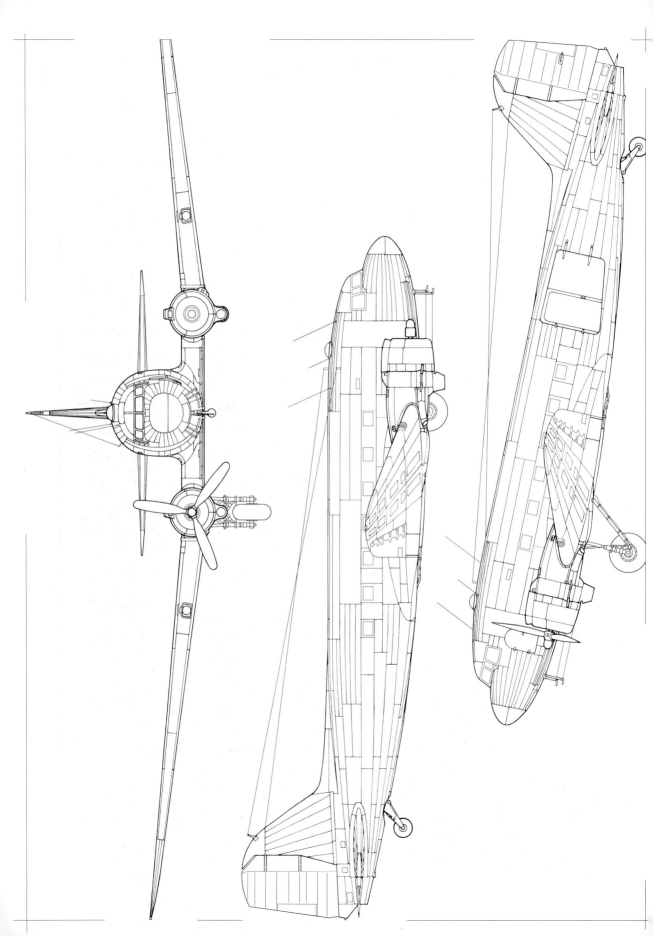

COLOUR PLATES

Notes

Earlier production and ex-airline aircraft had overall olive drab (OD) and neutral grey undersurfaces. Most C-47s had a factory-applied forest green pattern over OD. A few – mainly ex-airliners and early production C-53s – had forest green overall in place of OD. Some C-47s also received forest green overspray on the undersurfaces as well. The forest green overspray often disappeared when an aircraft was repainted. In some C-47s – especially intermediate production aircraft – green overspray was not extended to the fuselage, but only on the wings and tail section.

OD wore differently depending on where it was applied. The paint on the control surfaces always looked different, even when the aeroplane was brand new. This was because of the differing surface reflectivity, as well as the fact that the control surfaces were supplied, doped and painted by a subcontractor. The control surfaces, the fin, and the outer wing panels were where the most variation was evident. Some faded OD was almost a light 'milk chocolate' colour. There was often heavy wear near door hinges, showing different shades of OD and repainting or reinforcing with tape or sheet metal. Repair work was 'touched up' usually in fresh OD, but sometimes in other colours, and the use of cannibalised parts meant that few C-47 series aircraft were monochromatic.

Most, but by no means all, nose art was painted under the pilot's side window on the left. Most often, the inside of cargo doors was zinc chromate green. Aircraft dropping paratroops or supplies often had the jump door removed and a number chalked on the fuselage side to direct loading. ATC, the US Navy and the Marine Corps generally disapproved of naming aircraft, but this was some-times done anyway, even if the names were paint-ed out after being photographed. Policies and styles in units often changed. Some units named aircraft according to a system, at least with original equipment, although these often broke down with replacement aircraft. This included the 33rd TCS (Indian tribes) and 41st TCS (trains). This often led to multiple names on aircraft in the form of two names on the nose or a second name applied airline-style above windows.

Natural metal aircraft were originally limited to ATC, NATS and C-47s that had been through a major overhaul in-theatre. By 1945, they had become more common – units such as the 54th TCS, which lacked an air threat, stripped off all paint – but the bulk of C-47s and R4Ds were camouflaged into the post-war era. Natural metal aircraft normally had black (factory delivered) or olive drab (depot repainting) anti-glare panels. Natural metal R4Ds often had black wing walkways. Exhaust stains and faded paint demonstrated, from above, the intensive use common to most C-47s and R4Ds, which flew more hours than fighters or bombers.

R4Ds were generally painted like C-47s, as they were almost all taken over from USAAF contracts. This has tended to detract from their historical significance, as they were often assumed to be USAAF aircraft. Those overhauled by the Navy or Marine Corps were, however, sometimes painted like other twin-engined naval aircraft such as PBYs or PBJs. However, in keeping with Navy and Marine Corps practice, most R4Ds had no visible serial numbers. Where they did appear on the fin, they were often in small numerals. The main designation was the two-digit aircraft number.

The US-Australian Directorate of Air Transport, operating through 1942-44, identified all its aircraft by Australian civil registrations on the fin. Even US military aircraft received these markings, used as call-signs. On many aircraft, these were painted over the serial numbers. With the end of DAT, the FEAF attempted to continue a unified designation system, with limited success.

Unlike the ETO, there was no systematic series of code numbers. Throughout the Pacific and CBI, the most important identifier of a C-47/R4D was the aircraft number. This was a single- to four-digit number (sometimes preceded by a letter) by which the aircraft was known. In the ATC and some units (such as 1st ACG and 1st CCG), it was the last three or four digits of the serial number. Most aircraft numbers lacked this connection. The Fifth Air Force (and, after that, the FEAF) tried to standardise the system with blocks of numbers assigned to each group and squadron, but this was unevenly applied in practice. Following this, letter suffixes/prefixes were added to each aircraft number, intended to allow differentiation between C-47s and the increasing numbers of C-46s.

USAAF serial numbers were usually carried in yellow (black on repainted or natural metal aircraft) across the fin. DAT aircraft with Australian registrations sometimes omitted the serial. The Navy and Marine Corps specification normally required the serial (and the aircraft type) in relatively small lettering that was often omitted.

Squadron insignias were more common in the Pacific and CBI than the ETO. Many units were very proud of their insignia, and had decals made that they would apply over the names of replacement aircraft. Squadron insignia appeared on one (starboard side for 64th TCS in 1944) or both (54th TCS in 1943-46 and 322nd TCS in 1944-46) sides. Air Commando Groups were proud of their insignias. The 316th TCS of the 1st ACG carried five white fuselage bands and a question mark on the fin. The 317th TCS of the 2nd ACG had an exclamation mark on the fin. The 318th TCS of the 3rd ACG had a white tip stripe to the fin and rudder. The Combat Cargo squadrons in the CBI were identified by Roman numerals on the fin and variations of the COM-CAR designator.

The use of airline-style titles was much more common than in the ETO. Some of these were personal names. Unit designators were more common. These included 'The Great Snafu Fleet' (1st CCG in 1944-45), 'The Tokyo Trolley' (originally the 55th TCS, later applied to other 375th TCG aircraft), 'Imperial Couriers' (55th TCS post-VJ-Day), 'Jungle Skippers' (317th TCG in 1944-46), 'Bully Beef Express' (6th TCS in 1944-46), 'Tiger Fleet' (1st TCS in 1945-46), 'Smiley's Airlines' (15th TCS in 1944-45), 'Frontline Airline' (433rd TCG in 1944-45) and others.

Painting rudder trim tabs in squadron colours was practised in the Fifth Air Force in 1944 and spread to the Thirteen when FEAF was formed. These included 6th TCS (red or white), 21st TCS (white-red-yellow stripes), 22nd TCS (yellow) and 33rd TCS (white). Other squadrons had cowling markings (white ring and stripe in the 1st TCS).

Aircraft numbers were often painted on the nose (ATC in a white diamond) or vertically on the grey belly under the nose (317th TCG in 1944-45). This allowed the aircraft to be identified on a crowded airstrip, parked nose-on to the taxiway.

In 1944-46, ATC aircraft in the CBI would often add the name of their home base to the fin above the aircraft number. ATC carried its insignia on its aircraft throughout the war. NATS followed this practice in 1944-45, adding unit designators under the insignia or airline-style titles.

1
C-41 (serial and unit unknown), Ladd Field, Alaska, summer 1941
This was one of the first pre-war DC-3 family aircraft to join the USAAC. Basically a DC-3, it was based at Bolling Field in Washington, DC and used in the summer of 1941 by Maj Gen John L De Witt, Commander of the Western Defense Command, on his inspection tour of Alaska. A Spanish-American War veteran, De Witt was unsympathetic to the USAAC, yet by 1941, under his command, airmen had achieved their long-desired goal of permanent bases in Alaska. Note the C-41's airline-style windows, door and baggage compartment.

2
DC-3 NC33606, Hawaiian Airlines, Honolulu, Hawaii, 7 December 1941
This Twin Wasp-powered aircraft was damaged by strafing during the Pearl Harbor attack. The Marine Corps lost its R3Ds at NAS Ewa, while the 19th TS's two C-33s were damaged but survived and were repaired. Indeed, one was started and taxied to a revetment while still under attack. Within days of the raid, all civilian DC-3s in Hawaii were under military control, airlifting troops to the outer islands. This aircraft was used on these missions, and remained in military service until war's end.

3
C-53-DO 41-120051, Air Transport/Ferrying Command, Brisbane, Australia, January 1942
The first USAAF C-53 to go into action against Japan, this aircraft was one of five being shipped

to the Philippines as deck cargo aboard USS *President Polk* when vessel was diverted to Australia on 13 January. Flown by hastily assembled mixed USAAF/RAAF crews, this aircraft and another C-53 commenced operations on 23 January by flying US groundcrews into Java to support P-40 operations. '62TG51' also became the first C-47 series aircraft lost in action when it was strafed by A6M2 Zeros on Bathurst Island, Australia, on 5 February. It had made an emergency landing there the day before after Darwin was socked in, and had been damaged in the process. The remaining four original C-53s served on, however, with at least one retaining its 1941 national insignia long after all other combat aircraft had painted out the red centre.

4
C-48C-DO 42-38336, Assam Burma Ferry Command, Karachi, India, June 1942
This aircraft was flown in China and Burma by numerous crews, including 2Lt Bert Carleton (pilot) and MSgt Glenn Beard (co-pilot). A converted Pan American Airlines DC-3A-414, it had been sent to the CBI specially to fly the 'Hump'. However, the aircraft initially saw service during the evacuation of Burma. Carleton and Beard subsequently evacuated many of the Doolittle raiders (including 1Lt Ted Lawson, who had been a flight training classmate of Carleton) from China. 42-38336 eventually crashed in Karachi in July 1942.

5
C-53-DO 41-20073 *Butchie 2*, 19th TS, Seventh Air Force, NAS Midway, 8 June 1942
Transport aircraft were a critical part of the USAAF contribution to the Battle of Midway. This Hawaii-based C-53, flown by Capt Stephen J Rosetta, airlifted munitions and supplies and evacuated wounded from the island. B-26 crews flown to Pearl Harbor in this aircraft provided the first (inaccurate) participant press accounts of Midway.

6
R4D-1 '1' (BuNo unknown), VR-253, SCAT, Henderson Field, Guadalcanal, October 1942
This aircraft was one of the first 13 Marine Corps R4D transports sent to the South Pacific, and it was vital in re-supplying Guadalcanal in 1942-43. Like most R4Ds operating with SCAT in 1942-44, they were painted OD/neutral grey, with a two-digit aircraft number (and no visible serial) to identify it. Aircraft names were rare.

7
C-47-DL 41-18564 *FLYING DUTCHMAN*, 33rd TCS/374th TCG, Port Moresby, New Guinea, November 1942
Crewed by 2Lt George Vandervort (pilot), T/Sgt Steven Pitch (crew chief) and Cpl Kirshner (radio) this aircraft crashed near the summit of Mt Obree, in New Guinea, on 10 November 1942, killing six of the nineteen passengers on board. While some survivors were able to walk out from the crash

site, the wounded, and those that remained to tend them near the aircraft, perished. Rescuers had to trek to their location, finding no one alive, and a poignant diary on one of the C-47's doors.

8
C-47-DL 41-18573 *LADY EVE*, 13th TCS/6th TCG, Henderson Field, Guadalcanal, 13 January 1943
This aircraft was amongst the first dozen C-47s to deploy with the 13th TCS in October 1942. Flown by 2Lts Neal Allen (pilot), Louis Nelson (co-pilot) and Ralph Saltsman (navigator), MSgt John Rinaldi (flight engineer) and Cpl James Stanley Stratton (radio), it was lost on 13 January 1943 after leaving Guadalcanal en route to New Caledonia with 18 evacuees on board.

9
C-47A-30-DL 42-23582 *HONEYMOON EXPRESS*, 41st TCS/374th TCG, Port Moresby, New Guinea, September 1943
HONEYMOON EXPRESS was the lead aeroplane for the Nadzab airdrop (when flown by Brig Gen Paul Prentiss and Lt Col William Williams) on 5 September 1943, as well as several other early operations – including the second paratroop drop in the Pacific, at Noemfoor (flown by Maj H Waldman). Like all C-47s initially supplied to the 41st TCS, 42-23582 was named after a famous US train. While the name appeared on both sides, the pin-up adorned the starboard side only.

10
R4D-1 '5-R-105' (BuNo unknown), VR-5, NATS, Adak, late 1943
This aircraft was one of the very few R4Ds used by the US Navy to be resprayed in the service's distinctive 1942 two-tone blue-grey/light grey scheme. Typically, most R4Ds remained in OD.

11
C-47A-35-DL 42-23880 *SURE SKIN*, 68th TCS/433rd TCG, Port Moresby, New Guinea, December 1943
This was the first aeroplane into Finschhafen, New Guinea, on 18 December 1943. It had a pin-up on the port side under the cockpit and a mission scoreboard, the latter being a rare sight in the SWPA because of the large number of sorties flown on a daily basis when in New Guinea.

12
R4D-5 BuNo 17136 (USAAF 42-92842), VMR-352, John Rogers Field, Hawaii, August 1944
BuNo 17136 was another R4D to be repainted in US Navy camouflage, this time in the mid-war three-colour scheme. Originally used to train Marine Corps and Navy personnel in parachute jumping at MCAS Cherry Point, this aeroplane deployed to Hawaii in mid-1944.

13
C-47A-65-DL 42-100441, 1st TCS/443rd TCG, Warazup, Burma, August 1944
This particular aircraft arrived in the CBI at Karachi

in December 1943, and it was operated by the 1st TCS until damaged on 18 September 1944 at a forward airstrip. After being cannibalised for parts, it was destroyed in December 1944.

14
C-47A-80-DL 43-15366 *"THE GIG"*, 3rd CCS/1st CCG, Sylhet, India, September 1944
On 14 December 1944, this aircraft evaded an attack by a Ki-44 'Tojo' fighter south of Bhamo. Its crew on this occasion consisted of 2Lt John Martin (pilot), Flt Off Marshall Field (co-pilot), SSgt Ivan Damon (radio operator) and Pvtes D V Kientz, A N Fillion and J Ledue ('kickers').

15
C-47A-75-DL 42-100968, 319th TCS(C)/1st ACG, North Burma, November 1944
A participant in Operation *Grubworm* (airlift to China), this particular aircraft also took part in the February 1945 airlift to Meiktila and the May 1945 Rangoon parachute assault. It retrieved gliders from forward airstrips, using the retractable hook under the fuselage to snag a tow rope which was looped around two poles. Few 1st ACG ships had names until later in 1945.

16
C-47B-25-DK 44-75247 *WAUPUN WABBIT/ ALBANY NIGHT BOAT*, 11th CCS/3rd CCG, Sylhet, India, late 1944
Operating extensively over northern Burma, this aircraft was flown by Capt Walter Honan and serviced by crew chief TSgt Bob Padgett and his maintainers. The small white stencils on the stabiliser and under the wheels show appropriate safety clearances for pre-flight urination! This aircraft was used both for air re-supply and the transportation of personnel throughout the CBI.

17
C-47A-60-DL 42-24414, 33rd TCS/374th TCG, Hollandia, New Guinea, March 1945
42-24414 was repaired following a taxiing accident at Henderson Field in March 1945. The coloured rudder trim tab denoted squadron allocation.

18
R4D-4 '246' (BuNo unknown) *Back Bay Special*, MAW-4, Iwo Jima, March 1945
The insignia below the cockpit of this aircraft appears to be a personal one rather than a unit emblem (although some late-war Marine Corps transport squadrons had unrecorded versions of their insignia). '246' was one of the first medevac aircraft into Miyamoto airstrip on Iwo Jima.

19
C-47A-25-DK 42-93292 *ASSAM AIR LINES*, ATC, Sookeratring, India, June 1945
A late war veteran of the 'Hump', this natural metal aircraft operated out of the Sookeratring base that was cut out of tea plantations and a racecourse to become one of the CBI's most active

fields. The use of airline-style markings for unit/individual C-47 identification was more common in the CBI and SWPA than in other theatres.

20
C-47A-85-DL 43-15460, *CleoC/JUNGLE SKIPPERS*, 39th TCS/317th TCG, Camalaniugan, Philippines, 23 June 1945
This aircraft took part in the last parachute assault of the Pacific War. The nose number was painted vertically on the neutral grey rather than the more usual horizontal on olive drab presentation of other units – typical for a 1945-era 317th TCG C-47.

21
C-47A-70-DL 42-100792 *MARJORIE ANN*, 9th TCS, Seventh Air Force, Saipan, June 1945
This aircraft (flown by 2Lt Walter E Barnes) was part of the first formation to emergency airdrop ammunition to Marine Corps units on Iwo Jima on 3 March 1945. Other C-47s from this squadron were equipped for DDT spraying during the central Pacific campaign. The undernose 'luggage tag' marking was added in April-May 1945, this emblem being the insignia of the Central Pacific joint-service Transport Aircraft Group (TAG), which the 9th customised with its own 'The Victory Line' tag. Marine Corps aircraft just had 'TAG' written on their version of this marking.

22
C-47A-90-DL 43-15724, Alaska Wing, ATC, Ladd Field, Alaska, June 1945
The Alaska Wing, Air Transport Command, took over the bulk of air transport support for forces in Alaska after 1943. Among the Alaska Wing's 1945 missions was the airlift of priority Lend-Lease equipment to be turned over to the Soviet Union for its impending entry into the war against Japan. Post-war, this aircraft operated extensively in Alaska and to the continental USA and Canada with Brooks Air Fuel as N95460 until retired in the 1970s. 43-15724's abandoned hulk can be still be found at Fairbanks airport, Alaska, today.

23
C-47B-25-10 43-49023 *Traveler*, 27th TCS, Nanning, China, June 1945
The personal aircraft of Maj Gen Robert B McClure, Commanding General, Chinese Combat Command, 43-49023 brought the general into Nanning immediately after its re-occupation by the Chinese. It was later used to fly OSS detachments into China and transport liberated Allied PoWs.

24
C-47A-20-DL 42-23419 *BOMBER BARONS AIRLINER*, 5th BG, Borneo, July 1945
This natural metal C-47 was rebuilt by 5th BG from a 'war weary' C-47 for use by its own HQ flight. The 'Bomber Barons' had a C-47 for each unit, along with other aircraft, and they supported moves between bases, flew parts from depots and took personnel to Australia on leave.

25
R4D-5 BuNo 39057, VR-5, NATS, July 1945, NAS Adak, Aleutians
Flown by Lt Cdr John J Lawless and Lt 'Windy' Sommers, this all-metal R4D was typical of the aircraft used in 1944-45 by NATS in all theatres.

26
R4D-5Z BuNo 17224, Headquarters, Marine Air Group, Pacific, Shanghai, China, November 1945
This VIP-configured aircraft belonged to Headquarters, Marine Air, Pacific. Flown by Col Carson Roberts, Assistant Chief of Staff, 1st Marine Air Wing, it carried unspecified VIPs to China. The R4D's VIP transport status in the immediate post-war months is reflected by its lack of stains and wear. This aircraft was written off at MCAS Ewa, Hawaii, on 12 July 1946 when the pilot retracted the gear too early on take-off.

27
C-47A-80-DL 43-15397, 1352nd Army Air Forces Base Unit, ATC, Mohanbari (Assam), India, December 1945
ATC was years in advance of the 'real' USAAF in providing a rescue organisation. By 1945 there were several detachments of C-47s which would search for lost aircraft and, if necessary, drop supplies or parachute-trained medical personnel to survivors. By 1945 the Mohanbari detachment had several C-47s – mainly painted in variations of this one's high visibility-scheme – as well as light aircraft and even a few helicopters.

28
C-47B-30-DK 44-76458, 332nd TCS, Shanghai, China, December 1945
Marked with the 332nd TCS's 'three coolies' insignia, this C-47 was handed over to the Navy in late 1945 to become R4D-6 BuNo 50839.

29
C-47B-1-DL 43-16242 *TOKYO TROLLEY*, 317th TCG, Atsugi, Japan, March 1946
This aircraft was used by the 11th Airborne Division to make its first peacetime jump in Japan, and so marks the transition from wartime to the post-war era for the C-47. It had been passed to the 317th by its former owners, the 57th TCS/375th TCG, as units were disbanded or went home.

30
C-47C-10-DK 42-108868 *The Duck*, 54th TCS, Eleventh Air Force, Ladd Field, Alaska, 15 April 1945
On 15 April 1945, whilst being flown by Capt Doubler and 1Lt Weaver, this aircraft received damage to its floats that led to its conversion into a C-47A and further service with the 54th TCS. Another near-identical C-47C float-equipped variant was 42-92699, which served in Calcutta (reportedly with the OSS). 42-108868 was the only C-model known to have carried insignia, wearing 54th TCS Beaver decals on both sides of its nose.

BIBLIOGRAPHY

Operations

History of US Marine Corps Operations in World War 2, vols 1-5, FMFRP 12-34, Washington, January 2000, HQ Marine Corps
Stan Cohen, *The Forgotten War*, vols 1-2, Missoula MT, 1981 & 1988, Pictorial Histories
Wesley Craven & James Cate, *The Army Air Forces in World War 2*, vols 4- 6, Washington, 1983, Air Force Historical Agency
Thomas E Griffith Jr, *MacArthur's Airman* [Kenney], Lawrence KS, 1998, Kansas
Edward T Imparato, *MacArthur. Melbourne to Tokyo*. Shippensburg PA, 1997, Burd Street
Robert H Kelly, *Allied Air Transport Operations South West Pacific Area in WW2*, vol 1, Brisbane, 2003, Harding Colour
Stephen E Mills, *Arctic War Planes. Alaska Aviation of World War 2*, New York, 1971, Bonanza
Frank E Ransom*, Air-Sea Rescue, 1941-1952*, USAF Historical Study 95, Maxwell AFB, 1954, USAF Historical Division
Robert Sherrod, *History of Marine Corps Aviation in World War 2*, Washington, 1952, Combat Forces Press
Christopher Shores, *Air War for Burma*, London, 2005, Grub Street
Dr Joe G Taylor, *Air Supply in the Burma Campaign*, USAF Historical Study 75, Maxwell AFB, 1957, USAF Historical Division.
US Strategic Bombing Survey, Pacific War, Military Analysis Division, *Air Operations in the CBI Theatre*, (Report 67), 1946
US Strategic Bombing Survey, Pacific War, Military Analysis Division, *ATC in the War Against Japan*, (Report 68), 1946
E K Williams, *AAF in Australia to the Summer of 1942*, USAF Historical Study 10, Maxwell AFB, 1944, USAF Historical Division
E K Williams, *Development of South Pacific Air Route*, USAF Historical Study 45, Maxwell AFB, 1945, USAF Historical Division

Memoirs

James F Brewer, Harry Howton & Janet M Theirs, eds, *China Airlift – the Hump*. Paducah, 1980, Turner
Dr Carl Frey Constein, ed, *Tales of the Himalayas*, Bloomington IN, 2002, 1st Books
Jeff Ethell & Don Downie, *Flying the Hump*, St Paul, 2004, Motorbooks
James P Gallagher, *With the Fifth Army Air Force*, Baltimore, 2001, Johns Hopkins Press
Rudolph F Gaum, *Experiences with the ATC*, Gaithersburg, 2005, self-published
John W Gordon, *Wings from Burma to the Himalayas*, Memphis, 1989, Global Press
Col Edward T Imparato, *Rescue From Shangri-La*, Paducah, 1997, Turner
John R Lester, *Frontline Airline*, Manhattan KS, 1994, Sunflower University Press
Otha Spencer, *Flying the Hump*, College Station, 1992, Texas A&M
William H Tunner, *Over the Hump*, Washington, 1985, Office of Air Force History
George Wamsley, *American Fly-Boy*, NY, 1993, Vantage
Edwin Lee White, *Ten Thousand Tons by Christmas*, St Petersburg FL, 1974, Valkyrie
Monroe Withers, *A Texan in the CBI*, Green Valley, 1993, Green Valley Press

Unit Histories

Back Load (433rd TCG), Sydney, 1945, Halstead
Steve Birdsall, *Flying Buccaneers* (Fifth AF), Garden City, 1977, Doubleday
Lewis C Burwell, *Scrapbook: A Pictorial and Historical Record of the Deeds, Exploits, Adventures, Travels and Life of the 27th TCS for the Year 1944*, Charlotte, 1947, Lassiter Press
Hugh B Cave, *Wings Across the World* (ATC), NY, 1945, Dodd Mead
Michael John Claringbould, *The Forgotten Fifth*, Kingston Australia, 1999, Aerothentic
Michael John Claringbould, *Forty of the Fifth*, Kingston Australia, 1999, Aerothentic
John Haile Cloe, *The Aleutian Warriors,* Missoula MT, 1991, Pictorial Histories
The History of the Tokyo Trolley (375th TCG), Tokyo, 1946, Dai Nippon
Col Edward T Imparato, *374th Troop Carrier Group 1942-1945*, Paducah, 1998, Turner Publishing
Frederick A Johnson, *The Bomber Barons* (5th BG), Tacoma, 1982, Bomber Books
John R T Jones, *Pictorial History of the 322nd Troop Carrier Squadron*, c1982, self-published
Carmen Kight, *There's Rocks in Those Clouds* (433rd TCG), Lakeland FL, 2005, self-published
James Lee, *Operation Lifeline* (NATS), Chicago, 1947, Ziff-Davis
Oliver LaFarge, *The Eagle in the Egg* (ATC), Boston, 1949, Houghton Mifflin
Charles F Leons, *History and Reminiscences* (55th TCS), 2002, self-published
Lex McAuley, *MacArthur's Eagles* (Fifth AF) Annapolis, 2005, US Naval Institute
John G Martin, *It Began at Imphal: The Combat Cargo Story*, Manhattan KS, 1988, Sunflower University Press
John G Martin, *Through Heaven's Gate to Shanghai* (10th CCS), Ashland KY, 1993, self-published
Moresby to Manila via Troop Carrier – The True Story of the 54th Troop Carrier Wing, Sydney, 1945, Angus & Robertson
Capt John H Pennock and 2Lt James M Healey, eds., *Saga of the Biscuit Bomber* (57th TCS), privately published, c.1946
The Role of the Naval Air Transport Service in the Pacific War, Washington, 1945, US Navy
Malcolm Rosholt, *Days of the Ching Pao* (Fourteenth AF), Amherst WI, 1978, Rosholt House
Sky Train, Adventures of a Troop Carrier Squadron (67th TCS), Sydney, 1945, Angus & Robertson
64th TC Sqn, privately published, c1946
W E Smith, *2nd Troop Carrier Squadron, AAF, CBI, WW 2*, 1987, Cullman AL, Gregath
Two Years C/O Postmaster. A Pictorial Essay 13th Troop Carrier Squadron, New Guinea to the Philippines, Sydney, 1946, John Sands
R D Van Wagner, *Any Place, Any Time, Any Where* (1st ACG), Atglen PA, 1998, Schiffer
Gerald A White Jr, *The Great Snafu Fleet* (1st CCS), 2000, Xlibris

INDEX

References to illustrations are shown in **bold**. Plates are shown with page and caption locators in (brackets).